15.00

THE DACIAN STONES SPEAK

THE DACIAN STONES SPEAK

PAUL MacKENDRICK

THE UNIVERSITY OF NORTH CAROLINA PRESS
CHAPEL HILL

Copyright © 1975 by
The University of North Carolina Press
All rights reserved

Manufactured in the United States of America
Library of Congress Catalog Card Number 73-16210
ISBN 0-8078-1226-9

Library of Congress Cataloging in Publication Data

MacKendrick, Paul Lachlan, 1914-
  The Dacian stones speak.

  Bibliography: p.
  1. Dacia—History. 2. Moesia Inferior. I. Title.
DG59.D3M3   919.39'8   73-16210
ISBN 0-8078-1226-9

For
M. S. G.
habe tibi quidquid hoc libelli
qualecumque

CONTENTS

ILLUSTRATIONS

PREFACE

This book is the sixth in a series in which I have used archaeology to write cultural history. (Its predecessors are *The Mute Stones Speak* [1960], *The Greek Stones Speak* [1962], *The Iberian Stones Speak* [1967], *Romans on the Rhine* [1969], and *Roman France* [1972].) Its title does not precisely indicate its contents, for it treats the archaeology of the area of modern Romania, which embraces not only the Roman province of Dacia, but also Moesia Inferior, later renamed Scythia Minor. It ranges in time from the Neolithic Age (3000 B.C.) to the fall of Histria (seventh century of our era). I have been particularly impressed, as I hope the reader will be, by the competence of Neolithic sculptors and painters, the longevity of the Greek colonies on the Black Sea coast, and the architectural triumph of the Dacian citadels in the Transylvanian heartland.

The Dacian Stones Speak was a labor of love. I count it a privilege to have learned Romanian and to have enjoyed the hospitality of my Romanian hosts, especially Professor D. M. Pippidi, who twice allowed me to observe his dig in progress at Histria; the late academician Constantin Daicoviciu and his son Hadrian, who supplied transport, escorts, and lodging during my visits to Transylvanian sites; Professor Dumitru Tudor, who shared with me his photographs and his unrivaled knowledge of Oltenia; Dr. Adrian Rădulescu and Dr. Mihai Bucovală, who opened to me the resources of the Museum of Archaeology in Constanța, and enabled me to visit Trajan's trophy at Adamclisi; Dr. and Mrs. Petre Alexandrescu and Dr. Mihail Gramatopol, whom I have to thank for instructive converse over many a lunch at Coş, the charming faculty club of the University of Bucharest. Dr. Gramatopol also supplied the negative of the unique bust of Trajan in old age, figure 8.14. Thanks to these friends, the most satisfying reward of my work has been the discovery that in the world of classical archaeology there is no Iron Curtain.

None of these privileges would have been mine to enjoy without the introductions so kindly provided by Professor and Mrs. Edward Togo Salmon, to whom go my warmest thanks. It is a pleasure also to acknowledge the helpfulness of the librarians of the Institute of

Archaeology and the Romanian Academy of Sciences in Bucharest. In its late stages my work received welcome support from the Research Committee of the University of Wisconsin Graduate School. In sum, whatever is of value in this book is the result of international scholarly cooperation, for which its author is most profoundly grateful.

Rome

July 1974

ACKNOWLEDGMENTS

The author is grateful to the following individuals, institutions, and publications whose illustrations have been used in this book.

Alba Iulia
  Apulum: 5.4, 14
Bucharest
  Ion Barnea: 7.2, 3, 8–9, 15, 17
  Vladimir Dumitrescu: 1.12
  Radu Florescu: 7.4, 6, 18
  Mihail Gramatopol: 8.14
  Octavian Iliescu: 1.13
  Institutul de Arheologie: 1.3–11, 14–17; 2.4–8, 10, 16; 3.18; 4.2, 22–30; 5.12; 6.1; 7.12–14; 8.21–22, 24, 26
  Istoria Romîniei: 2.1; 3.1
  Monumentele Patriei Noastre: Emil Condurache, *Histria,* 2d ed., 2.2
  Dumitru Tudor: 4.14, 5.5–8, 11, 18, 19; 7.1; 8.1–2, 4, 6
Cluj
  Constantin and Hadrian Daicoviciu: 3.4, 11, 16; 4.1
  Institutul de Istorie și de Arheologie: 3.3, 10, 12, 14–15, 17, 19; 5.3
  Mihail Macrea: 5.1–2, 10
Constanţa
  Muzeul de Arheologie: 1.2; 2.11–15, 17–21; 6.2, 4, 5, 7–8; 7.5, 7, 10–11, 16; 8.9–12, 15, 17–18, 20, 25
Madison, Wisconsin
  University of Wisconsin Cartographic Laboratory: 1.1
Rome
  Deutsches archäologisches Institut: 4.3–13, 15–20; 5.17; 8.5, 7, 13, 19
  Gabinetto fotografico nazionale: 5.9, 13; 6.3; 8.3, 16, 23
  Anna Zevi Gallina, ed., *Civiltà Romana in Romania,* 5.16

The following illustrations were provided by the author: 2.3, 9; 3.2, 5–9, 13; 4.21; 5.15; 6.6; 7.19; 8.8

ROMANIAN PLACE-NAMES

ANCIENT	MODERN
Aegyssus	Tulcea
Alburnus Maior	Roşia Montană
Ampelum	Zlatna
Apulum	Alba Iulia
Aquae	Calan
Arcidava (?)	Popeşti
Argedava	Vărădia
Arrubium	Măcin
Arutela	Bivolari
Buridava	Stolniceni
Callatis	Mangalia
Capidava	Cernavoda
Carsium	Hîrşova
Cumidava	Rîşnov
Dierna	Orşova
Dinogetia	Garvăn
Drobeta	Turnu Severin
Durostorum	Silistra (Bulgaria)
Jidava	Cîmpulung
Napoca	Cluj
Noviodunum	Isaccea
Porolissum	Moigrad
Potaissa	Turda
Resculum	Bologa
Romula	Reşca-Dobrosloveni
Salsovia	Mahmudia
Sucidava	Celei
Tibiscum	Jupa
Tomis	Constanţa
Troesmis	Igliţa
Tropaeum Traiani	Adamclisi
Ulmetum	Pantelimon de Sus

THE DACIAN STONES SPEAK

1. ROMANIA IN PREHISTORY

There are people in Romania's history even more fascinating than Dracula and Madame Lupescu. This book is about those people in over three millennia of their history, from the elegant Neolithic sculptors of Cernavoda (3000 B.C.) and the potters of Cucuteni (2700 B.C.) to the heroic last-ditch holdouts against Slavic invasion at Histria in the early seventh century of the Christian era. Romanians have a claim upon our attention as inhabitants of a Latin island in a Slavic sea, as transmitters of Greco-Roman culture to the Middle Ages, as members of one of the most remarkably creative native states of antiquity, as victims and beneficiaries of Rome's last-acquired and first-abandoned province—Dacia—and as preservers, after Rome's withdrawal, of an amalgam of native and classical culture that makes their land unique among Iron Curtain countries to this day.

This book will try to bring the ancient Romanians to life against the background of their material remains: pottery, sculpture, villages, walled cities, grids of streets, civic and religious buildings, extraordinary citadels in mountain fastnesses, provincial towns after the Roman pattern, native villages that mushroomed at the gates of Roman camps, depiction by Roman sculptors of Dacians in battle and defeat, the blooming of cities along the Danube and the Black Sea in the late Roman Empire, the creative adaptation by native Dacians and Moesians of classical culture in religion, arts, and crafts.

Modern Romania's area is 91,671 square miles, about the size of the states of New York and Pennsylvania combined, or of England, Scotland, and Wales. If one superimposed it on the United States,

with the Black Sea port of Constanța over Philadelphia, the western-
most boundary would fall over Cleveland; in British terms, with
Constanța over London, the western limit would fall on the coast of
Galway. From south to north, the distance from the Danube south
of Bucharest to the northernmost point of the boundary between
Romania and Russia corresponds to the distance between Harrisburg
and Buffalo; or, in England, between Brighton and Newcastle-upon-
Tyne.

Sea, plain, and mountains comprise the geography of Romania.
As we work from east to west on the map (fig. 1.1), we find that the
Black Sea coast attracted Greek settlements as early as the seventh
century B.C.; this area became the Roman province of Moesia Inferior. Behind the coast, the plain of Dobruja slopes into the marshes
of the valley of the Danube, which here turns sharply north: the in-
tervening plain provided a passage for invaders, from north and
south, throughout Romanian history. West of the Danube, the terrain flattens into the Wallachian steppe, and the foothills of
Muntenia and Moldavia farther north; these areas remained remarkably free of Roman influence. The Danube forms nearly the
whole southern boundary, and throughout antiquity was the artery
by which the lifeblood of ideas and commerce flowed into Romania,
especially downstream, from the Roman west. Central Romania,
nearest the Danube, is called Oltenia; it flourished particularly in
Roman times. North of Oltenia is the mountainous and metal-rich
region of Transylvania, where the Carpathians are delightfully
reminiscent of the Berner Oberland. This was the Dacian heartland,
where resistance against the Roman conquest held out longest, and
where, between A.D. 106 and 271, Roman colonies and municipalities
flourished. West of Transylvania is the frontier territory of the
Banat, mountainous in the south and southeast, flat and sometimes
marshy in the north, west, and southwest. In Roman times it formed
part of the province of Moesia Superior; its population resisted
Roman influence without creating a distinguished culture of its own,
and will not be a major concern of this book.

The climate of Romania is what geographers call continental, with
extremes of temperature ranging from twenty degrees below zero
Fahrenheit in winter to one hundred degrees above in summer. Summer tourists visiting Black Sea resorts, which are in the same latitude

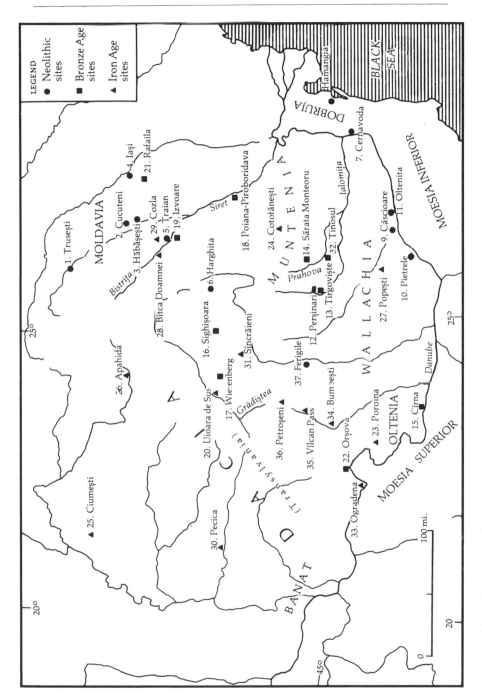

1.1. Prehistoric Romania, map

LEGEND
● Neolithic sites
■ Bronze Age sites
▲ Iron Age sites

BLACK SEA

DOBRUJA

Hamangia

MOESIA INFERIOR

7. Cernavoda

11. Oltenita
9. Căscioare
10. Pietrele
27. Popeşti

MOLDAVIA

4. Iaşi
21. Rafaila
2. Cucuteni
29. Cozla
5. Traian
19. Izvoare
3. Hăbăşeşti
1. Truseşti

Siret

Bistriţa

28. Bîtca Doamnei
6. Harghita
16. Sighişoara

MUNTENIA

24. Cotofăneşti
14. Sărata Monteoru
22. Tinosul
Ialomiţa
Prahova
13. Tîrgovişte
12. Perşinari

18. Poiana-Piroboridava

WALLACHIA

31. Sîncrăieni
37. Ferigile
34. Bumbeşti
35. Vîlcan Pass
36. Petroşeni
17. Grădiştea
20. Uioara de Sus
26. Apahida
25. Ciumeşti
30. Pecica

(Transylvania)

DACIA

BANAT

23. Porolna
OLTENIA
15. Cîrna
22. Orşova
33. Ogradena

Danube

MOESIA SUPERIOR

100 mi.

20

0

20°
25°
25°
45°

as Florence, find it hard to believe the exiled Roman poet Ovid's description of Arctic conditions: fish frozen in ice, wine sucked like icicles; but if they returned in winter, when the north wind blows sheer down from the Russian steppes, they would find he was only slightly exaggerating.

The country is generally fertile and productive; its resources in grain, cattle, timber, and fish attracted the Greeks, and its gold, copper, and salt made it seem eminently worth exploiting to the Romans. To both, it was a prolific source of slaves.

Romania's real history begins in Neolithic times, at an absolute date of about 3000 B.C. Neolithic culture in Europe is everywhere revolutionary: it marks the transition from a predatory to a sedentary life, from what a prejudiced witness would call savagery to civilization—the moment when man first begins to appreciate and to create beauty. But nowhere outside the Aegean basin is that beauty more breathtaking than in the sculpture and pottery of Neolithic Romania. In fact, it would be safe to say that the native culture had two high moments: once in Neolithic times, and again three millennia later in the age of the independent Dacian state (see chapter 3). One of the finest pairs of examples of Neolithic Romanian sculpture is the "Thinker" and his wife (fig. 1.2), found at Cernavoda near the Danube in Dobruja, and now in the new Museum of National History in Bucharest. The statuettes, in lustrous black terra-cotta, are less than five inches high, but they pack much in little. The caustic humor of modern Romanians would have it that the shrewish wife is scolding the patient husband, who is taking it philosophically. But there is more in these tiny masterpieces than that. Apart from the archaic realism, the simplicity of line, which any modern sculptor— a Henry Moore, for example—would envy, there is a spiritual dimension never attained in art before, and seldom after. The angular quality suggests carving in wood, but the closest analogies are the Cycladic statuettes of the same date in alabaster, like the harper from the island of Amorgos in the National Museum in Athens.[1] Either the Cernavoda sculptor and his patrons were of Aegean origin or

1. See Paul MacKendrick, *The Greek Stones Speak: The Story of Archaeology in Greek Lands* (New York, 1962), fig. 1.19.

1.2. Cernavoda, "Thinker" and wife, terra-cotta

there was already contact by sea, in the fourth millennium B.C., between the Aegean and the hinterland of the Black Sea coast, via the Danube.

The Thinker and his wife belong to the world of real men and women. There is evidence also for the divinities the Neolithic Romanians worshiped; for example, the statuette of what must be, from her exaggerated buttocks, a fertility goddess (fig. 1.3), from the rich site of Cucuteni in Moldavia, to which we shall return. The painted incisions on her body probably represent tattooing. She dates from 2700–2000 B.C., somewhat later than the Thinker. Partisans of women's liberation will be pleased to note further evidence of the preponderance of the female in Neolithic religion in the terra-cotta altar (fig. 1.4), a meter high, from Trusești, in the județ (department) of Botoșani. The taller figure is interpreted to represent the Mother Goddess, and the inferior one her male consort. Both wear massive necklaces intended to represent gold. The heads are hollow, and were presumably used for burning incense. Flat violin-shaped bone

1.4. Trusești, altar

1.3. Cucuteni, goddess

1.5. Căscioara, sanctuaries

1.6. Oltenița, woman with
vase on head

figurines of goddesses, incised to represent tattooing, have parallels in Troy I (2600–2400 B.C.). Another glimpse of Neolithic man at worship is provided by the terra-cotta model of four cult sanctuaries (fig. 1.5) from Căscioara, near Bucharest. It dates from 2700–2000 B.C., the same period as the Cucuteni fertility goddess. The pitched-roofed buildings, with their ornaments (acroteria) at the gable ends and peak, show an architectural sophistication not reached in Greek temples for another twelve hundred years at least.

A grotesque sense of humor is visible in the figure from Oltenița of a woman with protruding ears and prominent teeth, carrying a vase on her head (fig. 1.6), and in the anthropomorphic vase (fig. 1.7), extraordinarily like a Toby jug, from Sultana, near Bucharest, where the paint perhaps represents tattooing. An attractive sympathy with animals grins out of the tiny figure of a fox (fig. 1.8), less than two and a half inches long, from Pietrele, which was molded about 2000 B.C. Neolithic art in Romania portrays many animal figures, some perhaps totems: bull, dog, cat, stag, eagle, dove, ram, pig, tortoise, hedgehog.

1.8. Pietrele, fox

1.7. Sultana, anthropomorphic vase

The Neolithic flowering of Romania was not a sudden affair. Its gradual growth, from 3000–2700 B.C. onward, has been competently traced at Izvoare, some five miles east of Piatra Neamț. The settlement covers just over half an acre, on a terrace overlooking the Bistrița River; its rectangular huts, of wood and brush, contained hearths and storage pits; its finds include handsome pots decorated with yellow swirls, spirals, or meanders, painted under the glaze on a brown ground; figurines of steatopygous tattooed women; stone and bone tools; clay models of bulls, vases, chairs, and altars; beads, loom weights, stone arrowheads, spearpoints, axes, hand mills; chisels, hooks, spatulas, and hammers of bone or horn. Copper is treated as a precious metal: the little of it that the excavators found had been made into spirals, rings, and bracelets. Izvoare was a prosperous village, well-watered (its name means "springs"), blessed with fertile soil and plenty of timber. Its location at a crossroads made communication easy, yet, at the same time, it was protected by forest and swamp so that, until the Bronze Age, it escaped the attentions of marauding migratory tribes. It was the home of a single tribe, a tight, small, sedentary family community whose members were gifted with strong originality and a fine artistic sense. The figurines suggest a primitive polytheism; the female figurines represent the Mother Goddess, the bulls, the male principle.

Archaeologists and anthropologists name cultures after sites with rich finds that turn out to be typical. In Romania, the most impressive Neolithic site in all Moldavia (it measures 263 by 328 feet, and covers three and two-thirds acres), is Cucuteni, thirty-six miles northwest of Iași. The settlement lies on a rocky promontory-spur, sheer on three sides, 1,135 feet above sea level. It was discovered by accident during road-building operations in 1884. Reported by the pioneer Romanian archaeologist Alexandru Odobescu in 1889 to an international congress of anthropologists and prehistoric archaeologists meeting in Paris, it caused a sensation, which led to its excavation in 1909–10 by the Germans Herbert Schmidt (whose methods were unscientific, but whose watercolors of pots were exquisite), and Gerhardt Bersu, later director of the Römisch-Germanische Kommission in Frankfurt, who succeeded in establishing, by close attention to levels of finds, a series of phases (Cucuteni A,

A-B, B, 2700–2000 B.C.) that remain valid today. World War I and
its aftermath delayed Schmidt's publication of the finds—the most
remarkable Neolithic pottery in the whole Balkan area—until 1932.
Since then, stone quarrying, treasure hunting, and the use of the site
as a signal post in World War II have done serious damage, but
postwar excavation by Romanian archaeologists has been systematic,
scientific, and fruitful. The method, commonplace in Romania, has
been to drive a straight trench the long way of the site, widening it
at likely intervals. The result has been the discovery of thirty rectangular huts with floors of baked clay or stone slabs and horseshoe-
shaped hearths on footings of river pebbles. The walls of interwoven
branches covered with clay were made by the technique called wattle
and daub. Among the finds were tools in flint, bone, horn, terra-
cotta, and copper (for Cucuteni lasted down into the Chalcolithic
period): blades, saws, scrapers, punches or awls, chisels, and axes
both local and brought from the Aegean area, Asia Minor, and the
north. Terra-cotta loom weights and spindle-whorls prove that the
Cucuteni women wove on looms. Weapons were few (a scattering
of flint arrowheads and spearpoints), and the settlement unwalled,
yet a burnt level above Cucuteni B shows that this peaceful village
perished by fire at a date between 2000 and 1800 B.C. The villagers
probably looked to the sheer slopes on three sides to protect them;
across the neck of the promontory they dug two moats. The inner,
earlier one is from eight to thirteen feet wide and six and a half feet
deep; the outer, of phase B, is more ambitious: fifteen to twenty-
eight feet wide and ten feet deep. Stones from the trench were used
to reinforce its inner face. Late in phase B, the moats were filled in
and the settlement extended beyond: this expansion proved the settlement's ruin.

But the glory of Cucuteni is its painted pottery, some of it on
proud, almost overwhelming display in the new Bucharest museum
(fig. 1.9). The vases are arranged in the case in chronological order:
Cucuteni A at the top, A-B in the middle, and B at the bottom. The
selection reveals the variety of shapes and the knowledgeable way
the painter has adapted the design, often in contrasting zones, to the
shape of the vessel. Spirals predominate, sometimes broken, sometimes running, often oblique or vertical. The artists had a *horror
vacui:* they aimed to leave no space unfilled. Hence between the

1.9. Cucuteni vases, vitrine

spirals are painted ovals, circles, zigzags, triangles; even the insides of the vases were painted. The total effect, by pure but pleasant coincidence, anticipates early twentieth-century Art Nouveau. The clay is very pure, fired at a high temperature, so that it rings when struck. It was painted before being fired in the kiln. Sometimes the artist dipped his pot, before decorating, in a bath of colored clay. The colors are red, brown, or black on white, or, in phases A-B and B, white on the darker colors, with the designs outlined in black, or standing out against a crosshatched background of black or chocolate brown. A related motif, the angular spiral, appears (fig. 1.10) on the neck of a vase of the Cucuteni culture from Traian (department of Neamţ), southwest of the type site. Figure 1.11 illustrates in a close-up view the Cucuteni B vase near the lower right corner of the showcase in figure 1.9. It comes from Truseşti, and shows particularly well the adaptation of the design to the shape of the vessel: swags on the neck; diagonal zigzags and crosses, light on dark, on the body; and intersecting segments of circles, outlined in chocolate brown, nearer the foot. The whole ensemble of Cucuteni ware shows

a precision, an elegance, an innate sense of line and volume, a sure
choice of the happiest proportions, which entitles these nameless
potter-painters to rank with the finest anywhere, even in archaic
Attica.

The most completely excavated Neolithic village in Romania is
Hăbășești, between Iași and Traian. It measures about 400 by 630
feet, an area of about six acres. The village (fig. 1.12) contained
forty-four houses, which implies a population of 300 to 350, of
whom not more than 200 would have formed the work force that
dug the two protective ditches, each 400 feet long, from 12 to 24
feet wide, and from 5 to 12 feet deep. One moat required the moving of 2,400 cubic meters of earth, the other, of 970. The space between may have been used for pasturing cattle. The houses are
grouped around two larger ones: the arrangement suggests an aristocratic class structure. The open spaces around the chiefs' houses will
have been used for meetings: dances, the celebration of a new baby,

1.10. Traian, Cucuteni vase   1.11. Cucuteni B vase

1.12. Hăbăşeşti village, reconstruction drawing

a marriage, a funeral, a return from the hunt or from war, or an animal sacrifice, perhaps of a bull. (Horns of consecration, like those familiar from Minoan Crete, have been found on some Danube-basin sites.)[2]

The houses, like those at Cucuteni, had floors of clay (on which the villagers slept), and walls of wattle and daub, with very strong uprights of fir logs, four to six inches thick. The average size of ordinary houses with one or two rooms was thirteen by twenty-three feet. The clay platform of the house was built first on a wooden foundation; then the villagers built a fire on top of the clay to bake it hard. Pitched roofs helped to shed rain and snow; they had a wooden frame to support the thatch. Indoor hearths measured a meter square; some cooking was also done outdoors. Terra-cotta frames held hand mills for grinding grain. Perforated clay plaques, tens of thousands of sherds of which were found, were twelve to twenty inches square and served as home kilns for baking pottery. The shapes and decoration are the same as at Cucuteni; the pots are painted in three colors—red, white, and dark chocolate—sometimes with white motifs on a red ground, sometimes vice versa. The motifs

2. Ibid., fig. 2.18.

include running spirals, circles, tangents of circles, ovals, angular spirals, semi-meanders, zigzags, lozenges, triangles, and shapes like modern musical notes.

The excavators found tools and weapons, of flint, bone, clay, and copper (for Hăbăşeşti, too, survived into the Chalcolithic Age). Of over eight hundred arrowheads, some were found together with flint chips, which proved that they were manufactured on the spot. Some of the tools were made of basalt and jasper, not native to the region; they must have been imported from Transylvania and Harghita. There were blades, scrapers (for leather), polished axes, chisels, hammers (used by miners or stone quarriers), picks, hoes, spindles, and loom weights. At the point of transition between the stone and the copper ages, copper was a precious metal: the women of Hăbăşeşti used it for bracelets, beads, and pendants. They wore necklaces of pebbles, stag's teeth, boar's tusks, or shells. Hăbăşeşti, like the type site at Cucuteni, yielded both human and animal figurines. The human ones show tattooed females with large buttocks; the animals portrayed include bulls, pigs, sheep dogs, and wolves. The finds range in date between 2700 and 1800 B.C. The villagers were farmers, tilling their fields with bone plowshares, and raising grain, of which carbonized remains were found. (Hăbăşeşti, like Cucuteni, perished by fire.) They domesticated oxen, sheep, pigs, and dogs, kept in pens adjoining the houses; they fished, and hunted stags, wild goats, and boars. They led a hard life, a prey to enemies animal (wolves, bears) and human. They must have been allowed to evacuate their village before the final conflagration: the excavators found no skeletons. After a long gap, the site was reoccupied in the Iron Age (about 500 B.C.), and again in the eleventh century of the Christian era. Though now the spot is desolate, the taste and sophistication of the Neolithic inhabitants, revealed by modern archaeologists, have made it immortal.

The Romanian Bronze Age (1800–1200 B.C.) shows a retrogression from the Neolithic—at least in the technique of the pottery— but a number of buried treasures, of gold and bronze, testify to the wealth of the society, the competence of its craftsmen, and the precariousness of their existence. A good example is the Perşinari treasure (fig. 1.13). This consists of eleven gold daggers made from

1.13. Perşinari treasure

molds, in graduated weights, leading to the ingenious suggestion that they represent various denominations of a substitute for money in the days before coinage was invented (1800–1500 B.C.). The Perşinari treasure, together with a number of others of the Bronze Age and after, is on impressive display, under police guard, in a barred, vaulted, dimly-lit, red-carpeted room in the Museum of National History in Bucharest.

Molds used for casting axheads, of the Middle Bronze Age (fig. 1.14), found at Sărata Monteoru, seventy-five miles east-northeast of Perşinari, prove that some metalwork was done by local craftsmen, and not imported. Monteoru, the type site for Early and Middle Bronze Age culture in Muntenia (ca. 1700–1300 B.C.) is a settlement of rectangular wattle-and-daub huts on a terraced plateau, adjoining a great cemetery with hundreds of graves. The typical pottery consists of enormous pear-shaped sacrificial vases with funnel-shaped necks, containing wheat, elk antlers, and bones of horses. The pots were found in a stone-paved, elliptical sacrificial area with clay altars at either end. Finds of wheat, barley, millet, and stone sickles show that the inhabitants were farmers; finds of arrowheads show that they were hunters. In the cemetery, most of the bodies were buried in a contracted position, but some burnt skeletons suggest human sacrifice. Basket-shaped gold hair-rings find their match in Troy, while beads in faience (glass paste) and amber suggest trade connections with Egypt and north Europe. Bone cheekpieces of horsebits have Mycenaean ornament.

One of the most important Middle Bronze Age sites of the Danubian region is Cîrna, in a region of lakes and swamps. Excavation has uncovered 116 cremation graves. The ashes are usually contained in urns like the one illustrated in figure 1.15, with a bowl reversed as cover, and other vases within, or tucked under the cover, along with statuettes of goddesses, five to ten inches high, whose upper body is flat, while the lower part is bell-shaped. Among over five hundred vases, no two are alike. The décor includes incised spirals, meanders,

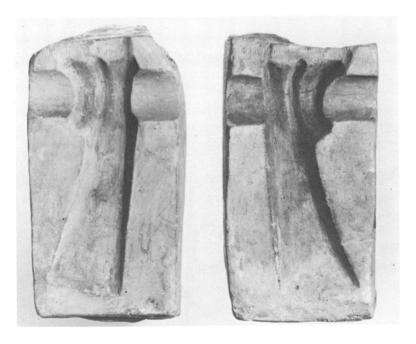

1.14. Monteoru, molds

1.15. Cîrna, urn

motifs cut into the fabric with a toothed wheel, and lozenge patterns. The burials show sharp class distinctions: over half are described as middle-class, while 15 percent are rich, and 5 percent very rich.

In Transylvania, the Middle to Late Bronze Age culture is named after the type site of Wietenberg (ca. 1300 B.C.). One of the interesting finds is a spiral-decorated hearth from Sighişoara (fig. 1.16), now in the Bucharest museum, whose motif is matched in the Late Bronze Age palace of Nestor at Pylos in Greece.[3] In sum, Bronze Age Romania grew to be as rich, and its craftsmen as competent, as those of Neolithic Cucuteni.

To the Chalcolithic, the period of transition (1250–1125 B.C.) from the Bronze Age to the Iron Age, corresponding to Sub-Mycenaean in Greece, belongs the tremendous hoard from Uioara de Sus, in central Transylvania: 5,800 objects, weighing over 1,100 kilograms and consisting of bronze swords, daggers, sickles, fibulas, pendants and fragments of bronze vessels and bridle-bits.

3. Ibid., p. 80.

The Early Iron Age in Romania is marked by a dizzy development of what Marxists call the forces of production. Fortified tribal settlements prospered on promontories, with a ditch across the least protected side. This is the period known to European archaeologists as Hallstatt (1200–500 B.C.), after a type site in Austria, near Salzburg; in Romania it anticipates the indigenous Dacian culture that flourished, especially in Transylvanian citadels, until the Romans ostensibly crushed it in the early second century of the Christian era. One of the richest sites is Ferigile (fig. 1.1, no. 37), where nearly two hundred cremation graves have been excavated, containing iron weapons ritually bent (scimitars, curved daggers, and axes), also characteristic fibulas and belt buckles, as well as harness gear, for men in the Iron Age in Romania, as elsewhere in Europe, were horsemen. At Poiana, in lower Moldavia (fig. 1.1, no. 18), on a plateau 650 feet high, with steeply sloping sides, just at the southern edge of the forest, where the steppe begins, evidence has been found of a Hallstatt settlement of the seventh and sixth centuries B.C.,

1.16. Sighișoara, hearth

planted on a Bronze Age site that had been abandoned for nearly a millennium. It was to become the Daco-Getic tribal center of Piro-boridava, important in its strategic, political, religious, and economic aspects.

One of the Iron Age treasures in the Bucharest Museum of National History is the necklace from Orșova (fig. 1.1, no. 22), made of linked bronze rings, to which are attached miniature jugs and a very fine representation of a wild goat (fig. 1.17, left). The fine bronze fibula in the same showcase (fig. 1.17, right) is from Rafaila in southern Moldavia (fig. 1.1, no. 21), and is dated in the ninth or early eighth century.

For our purposes the Early Iron Age in Romania is chiefly important as the harbinger of the flowering of Dacian culture in the La Tène period (the second half of the first millennium B.C.). To this we shall return in chapter 3, after recounting the fascinating story of the foundation of Greek colonies on the Romanian shores of the Black Sea.

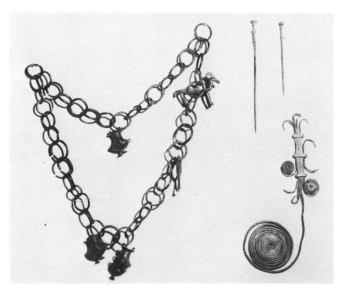

1.17. Orșova, necklace

2. GREEK COLONIES
ON THE BLACK SEA

One of the places in Romania where archaeology most agreeably writes history is Histria, on Lake Sinoe, a lagoon of the Black Sea, now landlocked; at the time of the colony's founding it was a sheltered harbor. It lies some forty miles north of Constanța, the ancient Tomis (fig. 2.1). It is a tranquil place, with luminous days and starlit nights. Herons stand patiently waiting for fish in the shallow waters of the lagoon, swans and gulls sail overhead; northward, under the grassy mounds of their necropolis, sleep the ancient inhabitants, Greek and native, of this Romanian Pompeii; within the walls, nearly sixty years of excavation have laid bare the streets and houses, the temples and baths of a city that knew nearly thirteen hundred years of history from its founding by Ionians from Miletus in the mid-seventh century B.C. to the early years of the seventh century of the Christian era, when it was sacked by the Slavs. Uninhabited since, it offers a fertile field for excavation. The same cannot be said for Tomis or Callatis (now Mangalia), the other two Greek colonies on the Romanian Black Sea coast: the prosperous port city of Constanța, capital of Dobruja, overlies the remains of Greco-Roman Tomis, and Mangalia, a flourishing bathing resort, conceals most of ancient Callatis. Histria, then, takes pride of place. This chapter will trace in some detail its history, and, so far as the archaeological data allow, that of its sister colonies, down to about 125 B.C., when Roman influence begins to become pervasive; chapters 6 and 7 will tell the story of Dobruja in Roman times.

When Vasile Pârvan, the father of modern Romanian archaeology, began to dig at Histria in 1914, the most conspicuous feature of the

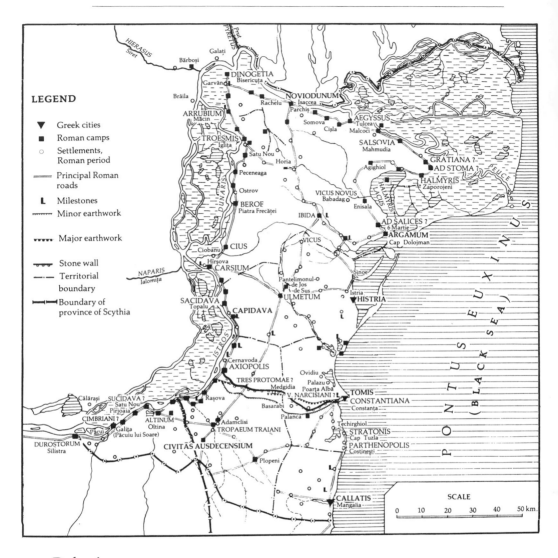

LEGEND

▼ Greek cities
■ Roman camps
○ Settlements,
   Roman period
═ Principal Roman
   roads
L Milestones
⌁⌁ Minor earthwork
▬▬ Major earthwork
▬▬ Stone wall
—·— Territorial
     boundary
▬◀▬ Boundary of
      province of Scythia

2.1. Dobruja, map

landscape was the late Roman wall (fig. 2.2, no. 7). It proved to be full of inscriptions in reuse, from earlier phases in the town's history, which cast a flood of light on political and economic developments, a veritable municipal archive. Pârvan knew from literary sources that Milesian colonists from Ionian Asia Minor had founded Histria, just before or after the middle of the seventh century B.C. (The precise date is controversial, and for our purposes does not greatly matter: some archaeologists use the pottery [of before 650 B.C.] to confirm Eusebius's foundation date of 657 B.C.; others allow for time lag and push the date down to as late as 625.)

Of the fifteen hundred inscriptions found in Dobruja, five hundred come from Histria, and there must be many more, turned face inward in the wall, which cannot be revealed without dismantling it. Furthermore, many others must remain to be unearthed in the intramural area, less than half of which has been excavated. Among the many things that the inscriptions tell us is that the Histrians remained loyal for centuries to their Ionian traditions: the dialect is preponderantly Ionic Greek, and so are the personal names; the constitution, modeled on that of Miletus, retained the Milesian names for "tribes" (city wards), magistrates, legislative and administrative bodies, cults and festivals, to the end of Histrian independence.

Miletus was the leading Greek state in the colonization of the Black Sea area, where the names of over ninety of her foundations are known. The motives must have been partly political, partly economic. The leaders of the Milesian venture to Histria, for example, may well have been disgruntled aristocrats who for one reason or another—possibly having to do with seesaw relations with their gold-rich neighbor, the kingdom of Lydia—saw no political future in the motherland. At any rate, Histrian inscriptions record a whole dynasty of ruling-class families, even after the Histrian constitution became ostensibly a democracy, about 450 B.C. The rank-and-file colonists will have been the poor and landless, eager to seek their fortunes overseas. Dobruja was fertile, the Black Sea and the Danube teemed with fish; in the hinterland the "barbarians" (the Greek term for anyone who could not speak Greek) early developed a taste for Greek luxury goods: fine vases, jewelry, olive oil, vintage wines.

The founder of Histria had a fine eye for a likely site with a good

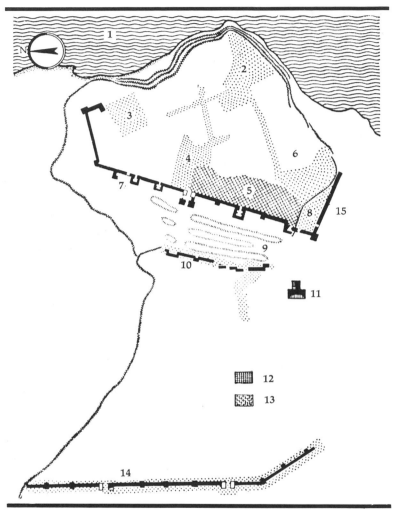

LEGEND

1. Lake Sinoe
2. Late Roman quarter
3. Temple area
4. Agora
5. Public buildings
6. Southwest residential quarter
7. Late circuit wall
8. Workers' quarter

9. Earthworks
10. Hellenistic circuit wall
11. Extramural basilica
12. Excavations, 1914-41
13. Excavations, 1949-58
14. Roman circuit wall,
    1st and 2d century A.D.
15. Museum

2.2. Histria, plan

2.3. Histria, temple area

harbor (it did not silt up until Hellenistic times [third century
B.C.]), excellent fishing, a fertile backcountry, and easy communication, across the flat Dobrujan plain, with native settlements and the
Danube only thirty-five miles to the west. He laid out a sacred area
(fig. 2.2, no. 3; fig. 2.3), with temples and an altar. Fifty-four humble wattle-and-daub houses of ordinary citizens have been excavated
in the area north (to the left) of number 10 on the plan. The
houses were humble, but the household equipment was not: in the
earliest levels, elegant Rhodian, Chian, and East Greek pottery; later,
in the sixth century, Corinthian and Attic ware. This inhabited area
of archaic Histria covered some seventy-five acres, adequate space for
a population of fifteen thousand. A burnt level dated by pottery to
the late sixth century B.C. gives mute evidence of the catastrophe
that put an end to this modest prosperity. It must be connected with
the abortive expedition of King Darius of Persia against the elusive
nomadic Scythians. Ionians formed part of Darius's expeditionary
force, and the Scythians presumably sacked Histria because it was an
Ionian city.

The colonists of Histria did not move into an uninhabited land. The archaeological evidence is that they did not subjugate the natives by force, but evolved a modus vivendi with them by appealing to common economic interests: each had something to give to the other. The Greeks could offer luxury goods in exchange for local grain, slaves, honey, wax, cattle, and salt fish. The evidence comes partly from aboriginal settlements in the backcountry like Tariverdi, not far inland, due west of Histria, where excavation has revealed a native village whose inhabitants made their own pottery, but also used Greek wares. Obviously the local aristocracy found much in common with the Histrian ruling class, and early adopted Greek culture. Also, there is something to be learned from the Histria necropolis. Archaeologists customarily discover much about the activities of the living from the tombs of the dead, and Histria is no exception. Excavation in the mounds of the cemetery across the lagoon, north of the town, has revealed much about the relations

2.4. Agighiol, treasure

between the Greek colonists and the native population. The tomb furniture of the burial mounds themselves is Greek, but the blood offerings in the trenches surrounding the mounds are aboriginal: skeletons of horses, evidence of human sacrifice, prisoners slain to wreak vengeance for the death of a chief—those were Thracian practices, not Greek.

Some of these native chiefs were very wealthy. The best evidence comes from the tomb of a Thracian prince, found by chance at Agighiol, not far north of Histria, and now on display in the Museum of National History in Bucharest (fig. 2.4). In the outer chamber were found the skeletons of horses, with the hammered silver plaques of their rich harness. The inner chamber contained the entire silver treasure of the prince himself: a silver-gilt helmet, a pair of silver greaves (shin protectors), with representations of human heads covering the kneecaps, a number of shallow bowls, and a splendid silver cup (fig. 2.5) richly ornamented with stags, birds, and fantastic animals. One of the vases is inscribed "Cotys," the

2.5. Agighiol,
silver cup

2.6. Cotofănești,
gold helmet

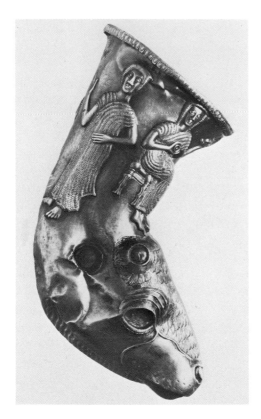

2.7. Poroina,
silver-gilt rhyton

name of a Thracian prince. Experts date these splendidly barbaric objects in the fourth century B.C. Another even richer find, also in the Bucharest museum, comes from much farther west, but will serve to illustrate the wealth of the native chiefs with whom the Histrian colonists did business: the helmet of Cotofănești (fig. 1.1, no. 24), of the same date as the Agighiol treasure, a chance discovery by a child in 1928. It is of solid twenty-carat gold, and weighs just over two pounds (fig. 2.6). It is decorated in the technique called *repoussé,* where the motifs are punched out from behind. These include rosettes; over the cutout for the face, a pair of huge eyes, to ward off the enemy's magic; on the cheekpieces, a warrior wearing a helmet like this one, his cloak fluttering in the wind, is about to slit with Scythian dagger the throat of a wild goat. The neck guard is adorned with two rows of fantastic winged animals. Yet another evidence of native wealth, from still farther west, at Poroina, near Turnu Severin (fig. 1.1, no. 23), and also in the Bucharest museum, is a silver-gilt rhyton (drinking horn) fashioned in the shape of a goat's head, bearing representations of goddesses, one standing, one seated on a throne (fig. 2.7). This is dated in the third century B.C., but some would call it later, by analogy with the Gundestrup cauldron from Jutland,[1] a Celtic work of the first century B.C. It probably came from the upper reaches of the Danube, the product of an artist who was at least dimly aware of Greek artistic and religious conventions, for ideas as well as artifacts traveled from the motherland to the hinterland of the Black Sea and the Danube basin. Yet no one admiring the barbaric splendor of these native treasures would mistake them for Greek work: the aesthetic control miscalled "classical restraint" is absent.

In Histria itself this is not so. The buildings of the sacred area, to which we now return, rival those of the motherland in workmanship, and many of the finds were imported from there. The largest temple, the first Greek temple ever excavated in Romania, used to be called Aphrodite's, on the evidence of a sixth-century vase found there in the shape of her sacred bird, the dove (fig. 2.8). But in 1963 the

---

1. Paul MacKendrick, *Romans on the Rhine* (New York, 1969), figs. 1.7a and 1.7b.

excavators hit upon a sacred pit, or *bothros* (fig. 2.9), where broken objects from the temple were reverently deposited. Among these were a number of sherds of Attic black-figure ware (late sixth–early fifth century) bearing scratched upon them graffiti that made it clear that they were dedicated to Zeus, the father of the gods. Furthermore, a nearby altar yielded an inscription to Zeus Polieus (Zeus the Protector of the City), which clinched the matter. Another significant find from the sacred area is a "Little-Master" band-cup, black-figure, of 530–520 B.C., which has scratched on it the graffito IEPH—Greek for "sacred" (fig. 2.10). Obviously it was part of the sacrificial equipment of some temple in the area.

The excavation strata show that the sacred area was burned near the end of the sixth century B.C., at the same time and for the same reason as the burning of Histria's houses, i.e., about 512 B.C., in the Scythian sack resulting from Darius's expedition. The temples were rebuilt, and burned again late in the fourth century, for unknown reasons: apparently the destruction befell them too late to be the work of Philip II of Macedon, and too early to be that of King Lysimachus of Thrace. At all events, the temples were again rebuilt, and there is three-dimensional evidence for two of them. One is a small marble Doric temple of which there survive fragments of the pediment, triglyphs (blocks with three vertical grooves), and metopes (plain blocks), and the inscribed architrave (marble beam from column to column), which records that the temple was dedicated by a resident of the north Aegean island of Thasos, with which Histria had close trade relations, to a mysterious Thracian divinity called the "Great God." The other piece of archaeological evidence for third-century temple building in the sacred area is the discovery of the foundations of a temple dedicated to Aphrodite. This time an inscribed cornice block makes the identification certain. In the forecourt of this temple was found a relief representing the three Fates (fig. 2.11), often worshiped with the goddess of love. The Fates sit on a bench, heads veiled, sacrificial saucers in their hands. They bear an extraordinary resemblance to the triad called Matres or Matronae, often represented on reliefs from Germany.[2]

Though no other temples have yet been found, there is inscrip-

---

2. Ibid., fig. 6.9, from Bonn.

2.8. Histria, dove vase

2.9. Histria, bothros

2.10. Histria, IEPH cup

2.11. Histria, the three Fates

tional evidence for the cults at Histria of the Ionian Apollo the Healer;[3] his sister, the huntress Artemis, and their mother Latona; Demeter, goddess of grain; Dionysus, god of wine; the gods' messenger Hermes; the Muses; and three gods who testify to the importance of seafaring at Histria—Poseidon, and the great twin brethren, Castor and Pollux, who also appear on the obverse of the city's handsome silver coins (fig. 2.12a). The reverse of the coin bears a dolphin—another marine motif—along with an eagle (fig. 12.2b).

Mention of these temples and cult inscriptions has taken us down into Histria's Hellenistic Age. Turning to politics takes us back to the middle of the fifth century B.C., when, according to no less an authority than Aristotle, Histria changed her constitution from an oligarchy to a democracy. This was apparently imposed by force, and may have had something to do with a Black Sea expedition undertaken by the Athenian leader Pericles: Athens was notorious for imposing democratic rule in cities where she had an interest, and she had a vital interest in maintaining the grain supply from the Histrian hinterland. While there is no surviving evidence that Histria was a tribute-paying member of the Athenian Empire, there is a good chance that her sister colony, Callatis, belonged (the name can be restored on the Athenian tribute lists); this creates an a fortiori presumption that Histria, a much more important place, was listed on a missing fragment.

Inscriptions tell us something about how Histrian democracy worked. There was an elected assembly and council; the vote was denied, as everywhere in Greek lands, to slaves, resident aliens, and women, but the inscriptions show that in later times Histrian women exercised important religious and civil functions. One woman is recorded as "never having refused a contribution or a service." As in the mother city of Miletus, a board of archons constituted the executive branch and a committee of the council directed its debates. A market commissioner regulated the price of grain and wine. We have a late record of one commissioner who erected a market building at his own expense; as a reward, he was twice reelected. No record of

---

3. Histrians reckoned dates by the annual term of his priest.

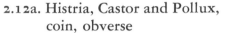

2.12a. Histria, Castor and Pollux,   2.12b. Histria, eagle and dolphin,
coin, obverse   coin, reverse

the workings of the judicial branch survives, but an inscription mentions a board that took care of the interests of orphans during their minority, somewhat like the Lord Chancellor's court in England.

Civil defense seems to have been in the hands of a citizen militia, sometimes aided by mercenaries and "barbarians" from the hinterland. The democracy undertook also the important task of keeping the city walls in good repair. We have a record of an official whose duties amusingly anticipate those of the "fence-viewer" elected at New England town meetings. These officials were responsible for the building of Histria's Hellenistic wall during the fourth to second centuries B.C. (fig. 2.2, no. 10). It was built of yellow sandstone, in two faces, with a fill of schist and with transverse beams for strengthening; it was provided with gates and towers.

Histria's walls saw a good deal of action. Philip II of Macedon battled the Thracians (348 B.C.) and the Scythians (339). His son Alexander the Great, who crossed the Danube against the Thracians in 335, may have appeared before the walls of Histria. Histria revolted against the rule of King Lysimachus of Thrace (313), and, when he put down the revolt, called him a tyrant; at his death in 281, the city resumed its independence, but may have suffered from invading Celts in 279. In about 262 Histria went to war against Byzantium over the control of the harbor of Tomis; she lost, and was forced to pay tribute. As the third century wore on, the Histrians began to suffer hard times: their harbor silted up, and recourse to agriculture in the hinterland depended on paying protection-money to a series of Getic chiefs with names outlandish to a Greek, like Zalmodegikos and Rhemaxos. During these trying times, Histrians often were forced to resort to the generosity of foreigners—from Tomis, Callatis, and Byzantium, for example—to bail them out of financial difficulties, as is proved by a pathetic series of decrees in honor of their emergency benefactors.

Greek cities did not ordinarily assume responsibility for the public elementary education of their young, and the Histrian democracy was no exception. But private education saved Histrian youngsters from illiteracy, as alphabets scratched on vases prove. And late inscriptions, of 200–150 B.C., show that Histrians did subsidize the physical and humane education of their young men, called, as in Athens, *ephebes* (eighteen to twenty-year-olds), and *neoi* (twenty-one to thirty-year-olds), who exercised in the city gymnasia under the direction of an official chosen from among the rich so that he could personally foot a part of the bill, e.g., for body oil and for mead for banquets. The young men were offered food for the mind also; they heard lectures from local and visiting professors.

Finally, the city fathers of Histria provided an adequate water supply. The aqueducts, the first ever found in Romania, may have been in existence as early as the second century B.C. Eventually, the city had three. The longest brought water from twenty-five miles away. The water ran in a channel made of forty thousand blocks of stone laid end to end, lined with a triple coat of waterproof cement, and covered with stone slabs. The aqueducts went out of use when the late Roman wall was built, in the late third or early fourth century of our era; nowadays, a mule cart laden with a 55-gallon drum supplies the Histria excavators with water.

Early Tomis is archaeologically very sparsely attested: even the evidence for its foundation is late. This is because Tomis, unlike Histria, had been continuously inhabited since its beginnings. Like Histria, Tomis was a Milesian foundation, but it was of the sixth century B.C., later in date than Histria's. It is now a prosperous city

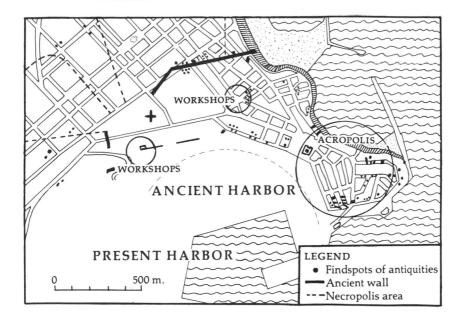

2.13. Tomis, plan

2.14. Tomis, early excavations

of two hundred thousand; it therefore does not lend itself to the complete excavation that is possible on an uninhabited site like Histria. For archaeological information about Tomis, we have to depend on chance excavation, when a new apartment house or hotel requires deep trenches. And these seldom go deeper than the Roman levels. Thus, for example, though Tomis has yielded no fewer than seven hundred inscriptions, they are virtually all late. We shall draw in chapters 6 and 7 on the epigraphical and archaeological evidence for Roman Tomis.

Meanwhile, we must be satisfied with what evidence we have. This is partly geographical. Constanţa today lies directly over the original Milesian foundation, on a promontory stretching southward, with ports on either side (fig. 2.13). The inner, western port was in the beginning, as it is today, the commercial harbor, safe and unsilted, to which argosies came from the motherland, freighted with luxury goods for the colony and the backcountry, and from which they sailed, laden with the grain and other commodities that the motherland needed: Athens alone, in 355 B.C., could absorb six hundred thousand bushels from the Black Sea area. The eastern harbor, today gay with yachts, in antiquity handled local commerce. Seventy years ago, when Tomis was a wretched Turkish village, it was possible to excavate it in depth (fig. 2.14), but the records of these excavations do not survive, and the history of Tomis is the poorer for it.

All we can do, for the first three hundred years, is to assume that Tomis looked and behaved like Histria, with similar walls, temples, public buildings, and private houses, that its people spoke an Ionic dialect (for which later inscriptions give evidence), that it was divided into the standard Ionian tribes (for which there is later proof), and that it was governed by the same sort of executives, legislature, and judiciary. The early evidence is so sparse as to lead some scholars to believe that until Hellenistic times Tomis was a mere appendage to Histria, but this is an argument from silence. When one is dealing with a continuously inhabited site like Tomis, the latest levels appear first, but this does not warrant the assumption that the site had no history below the levels that excavation has so far found. For example, it is reasonable to assume that Tomis, like Histria, and, as we shall see, Callatis, exploited its native hinterland, with which it had, as it still does, easy communications as far as the

2.15. Tomis, amphoras   2.16. Medgidia,
                                                   trophy sword

Danube at Axiopolis, the only lower Danubian settlement with a
Greek name; it lies only thirty miles to the west.

On the Danube near Axiopolis, at modern Cernavoda, excavation
has revealed evidence, like that from the Histria necropolis and from
Tariverdi, of close relations in the fifth century B.C. between natives
and Greeks. Native and imported pottery and jewelry were found in
the same grave along with a bronze mirror from Olbia, a Milesian
colony at the mouth of the Dnieper River; the mirror must have
come to Cernavoda indirectly from the homeland.

In Tomis itself, pottery in the Constanța museum gives mute but
eloquent evidence of early trade relations with the motherland: amphoras (fig. 2.15) of the sixth and fifth centuries B.C., stamped on
the handles with marks from the Aegean islands, Asia Minor, and
Thrace, and from the Megarian and Milesian colonies on the south
coast of the Black Sea—Rhodes, Thasos, Cnidus, Cos, the Thracian
Chersonese, Heraclea Pontica, and Sinope. Another piece of archaeological evidence for the relations of the Tomis hinterland with
the world of the Near East is the trophy sword from Medgidia (fig.
2.16), with a shape that must have come originally from Persia, as
the hook on the side proves, but the eagle-serpent motif is Scythian.

It is called a trophy sword because it was never intended for use in war: the back is blank, and contains a prong for affixing it to a wall, where it could only have served an ornamental purpose. A bronze cauldron of fifth-century Scythian workmanship, found in 1960 at Castelu, near Medgidia, gives further proof of "barbarian" settlement in the Tomitanan backcountry.

In the Hellenistic Age, Tomis itself was prosperous enough to tempt the greed of Histria and Callatis, who, as we saw, tried in vain to take over its port (ca. 262 B.C.). Further evidence of wealth comes from the Hellenistic necropolis, concentrated near the area of the old railroad station. The finds include a filigree ring, a necklace, and a spherical pendant, all in gold; bronze mirrors and fibulas, a ladle, a bracelet, and a diadem; an iron strigil, with which an athlete scraped the oil and dust from his body after exercise; and coins in silver and bronze, both local and imported. Pottery included a baby bottle and a perfume bottle, both from the same grave, which also contained the gold necklace mentioned above. There were also a number of terra-cotta statuettes, some imported from Tanagra in the Greek mother-land, some locally made, as is proved by molds on display in the excellent Constanţa museum, along with some two hundred of the statuettes themselves.

Finally, Callatis, now the Black Sea resort of Mangalia, some twenty-six miles south of Constanţa. Modern apartment houses, restaurants, hotels, a shopping area overlie the ancient city, so that most of what archaeologists have learned about it comes from outside the ancient walled area: tombs, buildings of late antiquity, and vestiges under-water of the Hellenistic wall and the port works.

Callatis differed from the other two colonies on the Romanian Black Sea coast in being not an Ionian but a Dorian foundation. Its original settlers came, toward the end of the sixth century B.C., from Heraclea Pontica, on the south coast of the Black Sea, which had been founded about 560 B.C. from Dorian Megara in mainland Greece. Callatis remained as faithful to Dorian traditions as Histria did to Ionian. Her inscriptions are written in the Doric dialect, her calendar used Megarian names for the months, her festivals copied those of the grandmother city, her coins bore on the obverse the head of Heracles, and on the reverse the club, bow, and quiver with which he performed his labors: stunning the Nemean lion, shooting the

Cyrencian stag, and the rest. The mother city of Callatis, Heraclea Pontica, was named after the strong-man hero, who was believed to have descended into the underworld to steal the three-headed watchdog Cerberus. Inscriptions and coins stamped with grain ears honor Dorian Megara's fertility goddess, Demeter the Apple-Bringer. The city magistrates bore Dorian names; her territorial subdivisions ("tribes") were Dorian as well.

But Callatis's loyalty to Dorian traditions may have been more apparent than real. Her ultimate foundress, Megara, fell victim to an Athenian embargo in 432 B.C., and there is, as we saw, some evidence —it depends on the restoration of a place-name on the tribute lists of the Athenian Empire as Ka[llatis]—that, voluntarily or under coercion, she became a subject-ally of the Athenian League, and adopted a democratic constitution. Her mother city, Heraclea, was ruled in the fourth century (364/363–353/352 B.C.) by a certain Clearchus, who had been a pupil of the Athenians Plato and Isocrates. He ruled as a tyrant; in the daughter city a democratic assembly elected the magistrates.

Since modern Mangalia overlies the civic center of ancient Callatis, we can only infer the existence of a market square, or agora, a Council House, or bouleuterion, and gymnasia for the training of the bodies and minds of her young men. But an inscription of about 200 B.C. records donations for the building of a theater, and inscriptions, coin types, and reliefs imply that there were, at least in Hellenistic times, temples to Aphrodite, goddess of love; Artemis the Huntress (fig. 2.17); Athena, goddess of wisdom, arts, and crafts; Cybele the Great Mother; and Zeus, father of gods and men. Artemis's twin

2.17. Callatis, Artemis hunting, relief

brother Apollo, god of music, poetry, and the healing arts, had at least two cults at Callatis, and in 252/251 B.C., a citizen of Callatis is recorded as one of the envoys who traveled from city to city to invite his fellow Greeks to Apollo's quadrennial festival at Delphi, the Pythia, which only the Olympic games exceeded in prestige.

Since Apollo's temple at Callatis, and the others, contained rich offerings, they needed to be protected by a wall. The one now visible dates from the Roman Empire, but it used, at least in part, the foundations and some of the superstructure of the defenses built as early as the fourth century B.C. The wall was made of beautifully cut blocks of limestone in two faces, laid as headers and stretchers, i.e., alternately exposing the short and the long sides of rectangular blocks. The space between the faces was filled with rough stones and earth, and weep holes were provided at the bottom of the wall for rainwater runoff.

Part of the Hellenistic wall is visible underwater from the garden of the charming local museum, which lies directly on the sea. Farther south, beyond the modern city, near the suburb of 2 Mai, breaking waves mark the location of one of the jetties of Callatis's port.

Equipped with a protected harbor, a sturdy wall, and a fertile hinterland, Callatis prospered in the fourth and third centuries B.C., despite the threat of Macedonian domination, a siege (310/309 B.C.) by King Lysimachus of Thrace, and the failure of her joint designs with Histria upon Tomis. In the third and second centuries B.C., until long after the deaths of Alexander the Great and Lysimachus, she minted gold staters with their heads on the obverse and, on the respective reverses, a winged Victory and Athena holding a Victory on the palm of her hand.

Bronze coins with an oared vessel on the reverse testify to shipping as one source of Callatis's wealth, while the grain ears previously mentioned testify to agriculture as another. An inscription perhaps of Hellenistic date honors a patriotic citizen who equipped a warship. A charming gravestone relief (fig. 2.18) portraying two children and a dog beside the stern of a ship adds another nautical motif. Only in the second century B.C. did Callatis find the burden of defense too much for her; she then gave herself over, like Histria, to native princes as protectors. Some of their family tombs, carefully built of cut stone, and vaulted, were found near 2 Mai; their rich contents included necklaces, earrings, and rings, all of gold. Inscrip-

2.18. Callatis, children, dog, and ship, gravestone relief

tions testify to commercial relations with other cities on the north
and west coast of the Black Sea, as well as with Byzantium, and
Aegean island ports like Delos, Rhodes, and Mitylene on Lesbos.
And of course she prospered, like her neighbors, from supplying
grain to Athens and Attica. Among the luxury goods shipped in exchange were large numbers of clay Tanagra figurines of the fourth
to second centuries B.C. from the border between Attica and Boeotia,
now mostly to be seen in Romanian private collections. Among the
subjects are a boy Dionysus and a Bacchante about to kiss him, an
adolescent winged Eros or Cupid, a phallic Priapus, Pan, a number
of hermaphrodites, a barbarian bearded lady, some comic masks,
several charming figures of children, and many toys: a dog, a ram,
and a horse four inches high, fitted for wheels.

The necropolis of Callatis, which, fortunately, lies in a park outside the built-up area, supplies further evidence of her wealth and
culture. Some of the bodies were cremated, others inhumed. One of
the cremation tombs was rectangular, in limestone, measuring twenty
by forty feet; it contained three cavities, each a foot deep (fig. 2.19),

in which the bodies were burned on the spot. The date is the late fourth century B.C. Children of the poor were often pathetically buried in the large wine jars called amphoras. An exception is a child of two, who was buried, late in the fourth century B.C., in a tile-walled grave along with three alabaster vases, and twenty-one tiny statuettes, hardly an inch high, in gilt terra-cotta, now in the Constanța museum. They represent dancing girls, Sirens playing the lyre, and winged Victories ("O Death, where is thy sting; o grave, where is thy victory?"). In addition, there are some fifty gilt terra-cotta rosettes, bunches of grapes, doves, Gorgon and griffin heads to keep off the evil eye, little gladiators (fig. 2.20), and beads, all provided with little bronze rings by which they could be sewn to clothing. The most interesting grave in the area was discovered in 1959 on a terraced slope west of the modern stadium in the city park. It lay under a mound forty-six feet in diameter, its circumference bounded with cut limestone, with a small altar in the midst. Vases date the burial in the second half of the fourth century B.C.; among the finds were fragments of a gilt bronze crown representing laurel leaves. What makes this grave (fig. 2.21) unique is the discovery, between the legs of the skeleton, of a papyrus roll, the first ever found in Romania. It disintegrated into fragments on exposure to the air, and the Russian "experts" to whom it was submitted for restoration failed in their task. If they had succeeded, the world would have been enriched with the oldest known Greek papyrus. Its contents are unknown; a papyrus of the same date, from a tomb at Derveni, in Greek Macedonia, referred to the Orphic mysteries. Whatever our papyrus said, its presence in the grave implies a cultured and literate intellectual climate; it proves again that ideas as well as commodities made their way from the Greek homeland to the distant Black Sea coast.

The Greek colonists of Histria, Tomis, and Callatis regarded themselves as civilized settlers in a barbarian land. Their Getic and Dacian neighbors came to appreciate the good things the Greeks brought: the olive oil and wine, the fine vases and jewelry, which Greek traders brought up the river valleys and into the mountains of Transylvania. There the ancestors of modern Romanians contrived to absorb the best of Greek culture without losing their own. The fascinating story of how they managed this will be the theme of the next chapter.

2.19. Callatis, *ustrinum*

2.20. Callatis, gladiator,
    gilt terra-cotta

2.21. Callatis, papyrus grave

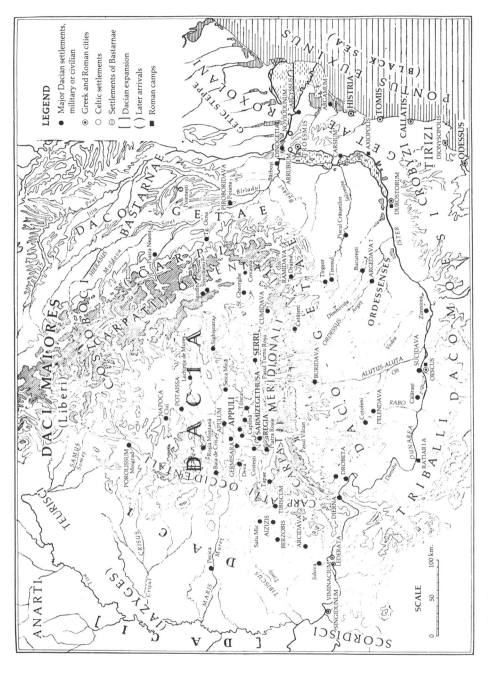

3.1. Dacian heartland, map

3. THE DACIAN HEARTLAND

The Greek colonists on Romania's Black Sea coast must have regarded the natives in the hinterland as "lesser breeds without the law," much as Kipling's British regarded the Indians. But the natives in both cases were more cultured than their culture-bound judges knew, a point that Romanian archaeologists have repeatedly and convincingly made since World War II. The natives with whom we shall be concerned in this chapter are the Getae of Muntenia and Moldavia in the eastern steppes (fig. 3.1), and the Dacians of the Carpathian Mountains. Herodotus calls them "the bravest and the justest of the Thracians," and they were in fact two branches of the same tribe, speaking two dialects of the same Indo-European language. We have met them already, in life and in death, absorbing Greek culture but keeping their own, in their village of Tariverdi near Histria, and in the Histrian necropolis. The story that archaeology will help us to tell in this chapter is of the development of the Geto-Dacians from a culture of rough, disunited tribal villages to a united state that reduced the Greek Black Sea cities to tributary status and held off the Romans for nearly two hundred years until Trajan finally crushed it politically in A.D. 106. But culturally it lived on, showing that unusual power to adapt to outside influences without losing the individuality that characterizes Romania to this day. The most fascinating chapter in this story is to be read in the citadels —veritable eagles' nests—of the developed Dacian state in the foothills of the southern Carpathians, in Transylvania, but these citadels had important predecessors in the plains farther to the east, and it is to these that we first turn.

45

The oldest known Getic site in Muntenia is Zimnicea, on a steep sandy bank above the Danube, sixty miles southwest of Bucharest, where the lowest level yielded sherds of Attic pottery of the late fifth and early fourth centuries B.C., proving early contact with Greece. Some of the reconstructions of early nineteenth-century peasant houses in the remarkable Village Museum in Bucharest will give an idea what ancient Dacian dwellings were like (fig. 3.2). They were log cabins, roofed with thatch or reeds, and containing enough hand-made local ware to suggest that the occupants were native though they imported oil and wine in amphoras from the north Aegean island of Thasos and wore fibulas (brooches) of bronze and silver that came from over the Balkans in Thrace. The excavators found burned levels that showed that the village, with its crowded and combustible houses, was at least three times destroyed by fire. After the third destruction, which happened in the reign of Augustus, it was not rebuilt. The final catastrophe was possibly the work of Augustus's

3.2. Zlatna house

general Sextus Aelius Catus, early in the first Christian century (A.D.
6–12), who, to punish the Getae for raids on Dobruja, by then
Roman territory, deported fifty thousand of them across the Danube.

As often in the history of archaeology, Zimnicea's cemetery is at
least as informative as the town. Five mounds were excavated. They
contained mostly cremation graves; inhumation was apparently for
the poor, for the cremations were of warriors, buried with their arms:
a Greek bronze helmet of the fourth century B.C., eight iron spearpoints, and a couple of Greek amphoras to prove that the occupant
could afford imported luxury goods. A male skeleton, in the same
level, buried without gear, may have been a sacrificed slave. Another
mound proved to contain, besides spearpoints, bronze arrowheads,
an iron bit, an iron knife, a gaming board, a Greek silver bowl,
Thracian fibulas in bronze and silver, a bronze bracelet, and an
amphora from Thasos. A female skeleton was buried with a piece of
local pottery, probably further gristly evidence of human sacrifice. A
third mound was dated in the fourth century B.C. by a bronze coin of
Philip II of Macedon. It contained the grave of a young girl, cremated and buried with her treasures: five gold beads, a silver pendant, a bronze mirror, and three silver fibulas from Thrace. A fourth
mound yielded twenty bronze arrowheads, and a coin of Alexander
the Great. The fifth mound was ransacked in the Middle Ages, but
the robbers left behind some bronze three-barbed arrowheads and an
iron battle-ax.

Faced with the contents of the Zimnicea necropolis, one can easily
call up to the mind's eye a local dignitary, a Getic noble, from one
of the larger and more pretentious houses of the town, not a worker,
but one who had others work for him. We can imagine him coming
down with his wife to the river bank to greet a Greek merchant ship
moored stern-on to the shore. He wears a mantle of expensive Greek
cloth, pinned at the shoulder with a shiny iron brooch. A short sword
hangs at his left side; over his shoulder he wears his bow and quiver,
filled with deadly three-barbed bronze arrows. His wife wears expensive jewelry: silver rings and necklaces, a bronze bracelet. A
slave accompanies them to carry their purchases. The master buys,
perhaps, an amphora of the aromatic wine of Chios, another of the
prized olive oil of Athens, and some elegant Attic red-figured vases.
What he has to offer in return are furs or grain; the Greek gives him

his change in Macedonian or Thracian silver, stamped with the heads of Philip, Alexander, or Lysimachus.[1]

The easternmost of the known Getic settlements in Muntenia, whose history goes back to the third century B.C., is Piscul Crăsanilor, thirty miles northeast of Bucharest, on the Ialomița River (fig. 3.1). It is a village of wattle-and-daub houses, in which the finds included an iron trident, bronze bracelets and necklaces of local manufacture, amphoras imported from the islands of Thasos, Rhodes, and Cos, glassware, beads of glass and gold leaf, the head of a bronze statuette, an elegant bronze three-wick lamp, and silver four-drachma pieces of Roman Macedonia, which guarantee that the site was still flourishing in the second century B.C. The town was evacuated, for unknown reasons, in the first century B.C. In its two centuries of history it may have had one moment of glory: it may have been here that the Getic chief Dromichaetes held Lysimachus, king of Thrace, prisoner in 292 B.C.

The richest and most important Geto-Dacian site in Muntenia is Popești, thirteen miles southwest of Bucharest (Argedava? on the map, fig. 3.1). It flourished in the second and first centuries B.C., behind an earthwork that had been made more resistant by the building of a fire against the outer face to harden the clay. Later, the inhabitants heightened the earthwork with a palisade. The houses were made of wood or wattle and daub, some of the former with tile roofs, a refinement borrowed from the Greeks. Most important was a chief's house, with a complex of walls and corridors that caused the excavator to dignify it with the name of "palace," and to conjecture that Popești, perhaps then called Argedava, was the capital of the Dacian tribal union before Burebista, the first great Dacian king, moved to the Transylvanian foothills, probably shortly before 80 B.C., leaving Popești to carry on for another two or three generations as just another Dacian village. Adjoining the "palace" was a "temple," an apsidal building with forecourt and cella, and ceremonial hearths, one decorated with a wave pattern, as at Sighișoara (fig. 1.16). Workshops with kilns and pottery molds, smiths' tools, and

1. I owe this vivid piece of reporting to Hadrian Daicoviciu, *Dacii* (Bucharest, 1968), p. 51.

many loom weights give evidence of local crafts. The excavator thought that some of the sherds (ostraca) he found had been used, in this "military democracy," for voting, as was done by the Athenians when they "ostracized" a fellow citizen.

The finds from Popești are extremely rich. There is local pottery, both hand- and wheel-made, imitating Greek shapes; also imported Hellenistic ware, and amphoras from Rhodes and Cos. The local imitations of these have nonalphabetic stamps impressed on the handles, which suggests that the townsfolk of Popești were, in whole or in part, illiterate. There are hand mills, mortars, whetstones, flints for striking fire; knife handles and cosmetic jars of bone; numerous iron weapons and tools: plowshares, hoes, sickles, shears, haying-forks, keys, chain links, nails, spikes, fishhooks, adzes, axes, chisels, awls, and tongs; and, from the necropolis, a folded shirt of chain mail, a Celtic sword, and a curved Illyrian dagger. There is harness gear: buckles, spurs, and bits. Jewelry abounds: glass beads, a gold pendant-medallion of the snaky-haired Medusa, an Egyptian amulet portraying Bes, the comic dwarf-god, pot-bellied, bow-legged, with protruding tongue and leopard's tail, who protected the wearer against the evil eye. There were bronze rings, necklaces, dress ornaments, bracelets, earrings, native fibulas in bronze, iron, and silver, and silver spirals, pendants, earrings, and snake-headed bracelets. There are coins of Thasos, Philip II, and Lysimachus; also local imitations, on which Greek representational art is metamorphosed into Geto-Dacian abstractions. The Illyrian dagger mentioned above is evidence for trade with the West; so are coins from Dyrrhachium (modern Durrës, Albania) on the Adriatic coast, and, sinister portent of future conquest, military as well as economic, Roman silver *denarii*. And in fact Roman legions followed Roman trade: a burnt level dated in the early years of the Christian era suggests that Popești, like Zimnicea, fell victim to the vengeance of Aelius Catus.

Two other Muntenian sites deserve mention here. The first is Cetățeni, on the south slope of the Carpathians some sixty miles north-northwest of Popești, and dependent upon it. Here were found an apsidal building with a priest's grave, and rock-cut libation basins, to testify to Dacian piety; amphoras from Rhodes, Cos, and Cnidus; imitation Macedonian tetradrachms, and Roman silver denarii, to testify to trade relations; iron tools, chain mail, and shield-bosses, to testify to local craft activity; a little gold jewelry, more silver, much bronze, to testify to modest prosperity. Cetățeni lasted longer than Popești: Aelius Catus's vengeance did not penetrate the mountains. But traffic shifted to another pass and prosperity declined.

Second, Tinosul (fig. 1.1, no. 32), on the Prahova River nine miles south of Ploiești. Since the region is poor in stone, both its palisade and its houses are wattle and daub. Its workmen made tools; its women wore bronze jewelry. Some housewives were the proud possessors of vessels of the imported Roman polychrome glass called *millefiori*. During the Roman Emperor Domitian's Dacian War (A.D. 85–89) Tinosul was burned, as a part of the Roman strategy that made Muntenia a no-man's-land; by the end of the century it was all Roman-occupied territory.

The Geto-Dacians absorbed another influence, besides the Greek, the Illyrian, and the Roman. This was Celtic, and it came down from the northwest in the early third century B.C. Some of the Celts stayed and dominated northern Transylvania in the third and second centuries. Some swept on into Greece, where they raided Apollo's shrine at Delphi (279 B.C.). Some entered central Asia Minor, where they exacted protection money and settled down in the region called Galatia after the Gaul they came from: St. Paul wrote a letter to their descendants.

The Celts who stayed in Romania worked out a modus vivendi with the Dacians in Transylvania, much like the relation between the Etruscan elite and the native Villanovans in Italy three centuries earlier. Romanian archaeologists count some seventy Celtic sites in Transylvania, but in most, if not all, of these sites (they are usually cemeteries; there were very few settlements), the finds show that the native population imitated Celtic art forms that took their fancy, but remained obstinately and fundamentally Dacian in their culture. By the end of the second century B.C. Celtic influence has faded: the intruders have either withdrawn in the face of the growing power of the Dacian state, or they have intermarried and been absorbed. A symbol of the Celtic-Dacian interrelation is, for example, a Dacian handmade pot with a Celtic wheel-turned cover. It was probably the Celts who taught Dacian die-makers how to make abstractions out of the representational figures on Macedonian coins: the same tendency is visible on Celtic coins from Gaul.

3.3. Ciumeşti, Celtic helmet

As long ago as 1900, the village schoolmaster of Apahida (fig. 1.1, no. 26), some nine miles east of Cluj, the capital of Transylvania, discovered a Celtic cremation cemetery there, with twenty-one burials. Since then, at least thirty more have been destroyed; the total makes one of the largest Celtic sites in Transylvania. Even here the burial rites show the presence of a local population. The graves hold Dacian handmade vases as well as Celtic animal sacrifice, jewelry, and artifacts. One of the graves must have been that of a Celtic prince: it contained a bronze helmet overlaid with gold leaf.

But the most spectacular Celtic find in Romania turned up by chance in 1961 in a sandpit near the far northwestern village of Ciumeşti, close to the Hungarian border (fig. 1.1, no. 25). The find-spot turned out to be another Celtic necropolis; the chance find was a splendid bird-crested Celtic bronze helmet (fig. 3.3), together with a pair of bronze greaves, an iron spearpoint, and a rolled and folded piece of chain mail decorated with bronze rosettes. Since there was no trace of cremation and no skeleton, the armor must have been deposited in the cenotaph of a prince who died in battle, his body not recovered. The prize piece is the helmet, half-round, with a neck protector. It was hammered out of a single bronze plate, with the cheekpieces bolted on. Through the top of the helmet protrudes a bronze spike, to which is fixed the cylinder on which the bird perches. The legs and the underpart of the head are cast, the rest is hammered. The eyes are yellow ivory, the pupil red enamel, fastened in with bitumen. The beak, which is restored, was probably also ivory. The right wing was repaired in antiquity: it bears a different wave pattern from the left. The claws, separately cast, are fastened to the perch with a removable iron nail. The bird is thirteen inches long; its wingspread is nine inches. The technique shows long experience in metalworking. The bird, whether raven, eagle, or falcon, is obviously a totem: a coin type shows a warrior wearing a wild boar crest on his helmet, and there is a bird crest on the Gundestrup cauldron, now in Copenhagen.[2] The date of the Ciumeşti helmet is controversial: the necropolis was in use from about 230 to 130 B.C., but the helmet could be an heirloom. In any case, it is among the oldest Celtic finds in Romania. It is now on display in the Museum of National History in Bucharest, where it symbolizes the fruitful effect on ancient Romanians of contact with another culture with a different and perhaps superior aesthetic ideal.

Dacian sites, as archaeology reveals them, begin to show signs of increased prosperity in the course of the first century B.C. The flesh-and-blood reason for this, the first three-dimensional person of whom we hear in Dacian history, was the Geto-Dacian king Burebista, who by diplomatic and military genius, by persuasion and force of arms, contrived to unite the hitherto divided native tribes between Pannonia and the Black Sea, and southward into Thrace. He imposed his will ruthlessly upon the Greek colonies on the Black Sea coast. He was almost equally severe with his own people, forcing them to uproot their grapevines in order, we are told, to reduce their lamentable tendency to drunkenness. In his moral endeavors, he had the help of his high priest, Deceneus. As we saw, probably sometime between 89 and 80 B.C., he moved his capital from Popeşti to the southern Carpathians. As the strongest power north of the Balkan Mountains,

2. MacKendrick, *Romans on the Rhine*, p. 16.

he was courted by Pompey, who wanted his help against Caesar in
Rome's civil war of 49–45 B.C. But Pompey was beaten, and Caesar
was planning an expedition against Burebista when the assassins'
daggers struck him down in 44. Unfortunately for Dacian unity,
Burebista was murdered in the same year by jealous tribal chiefs
chafing under his autocratic rule. At his death his kingdom broke up
into four or five parts—though its Transylvanian nucleus remained—
and stayed divided for one hundred years until it was reunited under
another Romanian national hero, Decebalus.

The Dacian heartland in the foothills of the southern Carpathians
(fig. 3.4), to which Burebista transferred his capital, is blessed with
some of the most entrancing scenery in Europe. The view from the
acropolis of Costeşti, 1,840 feet above sea level, commands to the
north the Grădiştea valley, and to the south (fig. 3.5) a vista that
can be matched only in the gentler parts of the Berner Oberland.
In the foreground of figure 3.5 can be seen orchards of plum trees
from which the delicious Romanian plum brandy called *ţuica* is
made, and nowhere more mellowly than here. Beyond are the steeply
tilted green hills, like Alpine meadows, where the sheep feed in summer. In the middle distance are forests of evergreens and oaks, which
in Burebista's time supplied the timber for strengthening the walls
of his citadels. And on the horizon are the higher mountains, rising
to 6,000 feet, which Decebalus relied on in vain to protect his eagle's
nest from the fearsome onslaught of Trajan's legions.

In modern times, interest in the Dacian heartland was aroused
early in the nineteenth century by the discovery of a hoard of gold
coins at Grădiştea Muncelului (ancient Sarmizegethusa Dacica or
Sarmizegethusa Regia, the holy of holies of Burebista's and Decebalus's kingdom). Transylvania being then part of the Hapsburg
Empire, Austrian engineers began burrowing for more, doing considerable harm by their unscientific methods. Systematic excavaton
began in the 1920s under the direction of Professor D. M. Teodorescu of the University of Cluj. Under the auspices of the Romanian Academy of Sciences, the Historical Institute of Cluj, led by
Constantin and Hadrian Daicoviciu, father and son, has carried on
the work. Teodorescu's old foreman, now over eighty, symbolizes the
continuity of the dig. He still lives in his farmhouse, embowered in
plum trees, on the hillside under Costeşti. Sitting on his veranda at

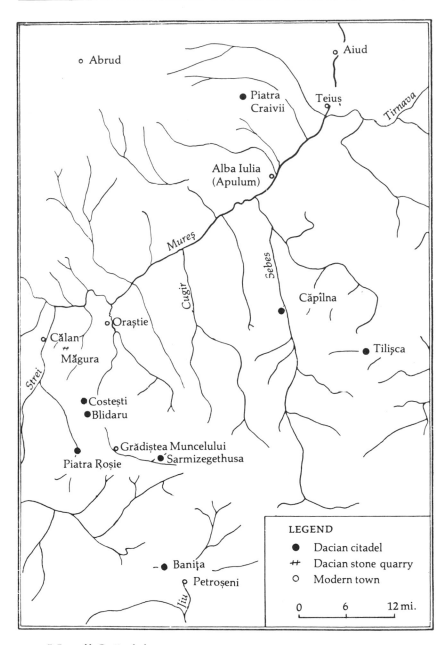

3.4. Munţii Orăştiei area, map

3.5. Costeşti, view to south

sunset, a glass of ţuica in hand, after a day spent exploring the site, is an experience that reminds one that archaeology can be one of the world's pleasanter pursuits.

The Cluj explorers have made the dirt fly in the Munţii Orăştiei area (the modern name for the Dacian heartland). For simplicity's sake, we shall concentrate on five sites: Costeşti, Burebista's acropolis; Blidaru, a typical fortress; Piatra Roşie, a larger citadel; Feţele Albe, noteworthy for its terraces; and Sarmizegethusa Dacica itself, the Dacian religious center and city of refuge.

First, Costeşti. It was planned as a stronghold commanding the river valley. An earthwork, twenty to twenty-six feet thick at the base, and still standing six to eight feet high, follows the contours of the hill, enclosing an area of about thirty acres. A palisade of stout oak logs originally topped the earthwork. Within it ran a towered stone wall, reinforced with sturdy wooden crossbeams to hold the two faces of the wall together, making what the Romans called a *murus Dacicus*. The cuttings for the beams can still be seen in the

3.6. Costeşti, *murus Dacicus*

preserved courses of the wall (fig. 3.6). Within the wall has been excavated a series of watchtowers. One, stone-built, overlooks the river hundreds of feet below. A second, near the middle of the area, stood on wooden stilts set in stone footings. The third is the most interesting. It is a two-storied tower house (fig. 3.7), approached by a monumental stone stair, with a storeroom below and living quarters above. The excavators think this was Burebista's royal residence. It is certainly more impressive than the so-called palace at Popeşti. The other remarkable find at Costeşti is a series of columned sanctuaries (fig. 3.8), one inside the walled area, and three outside. These turn out to be characteristic of Dacian sites. The columns seem to come in multiples of six, having something to do with the Dacian six-day week. The stone column-drums are never carried up to any great height, and they never carried, a roof. The sanctuaries were open to the sun, and were probably used for sun worship. The columns were either finished upward in wood, or the stone drums were carried up to a convenient height and their top surface used for burning incense.

3.7. Costeşti, tower house

3.8. Costeşti, sanctuary

Also outside the wall was a series of cisterns to catch rainwater for the use of the garrison and royal retinue. The Romans destroyed Costeşti in the First Dacian War (A.D. 102). Decebalus rebuilt it; the Romans destroyed it again in the Second (106), and it was never rebuilt.

On the far side of a hill within eyeshot to the south of Costeşti rises the imposing double citadel of Blidaru, 2,306 feet above sea level, a steep forty-minute climb from the river bank. The older citadel is the higher, trapezoidal in shape, the technique of the walls like that of Costeşti, with towers at the four corners. The entrance is through the southwest tower (fig. 3.9). Within is a tower house of stone and wood, not so elegant as the one at Costeşti, more suitable for a camp commander than a king. The second citadel was built on to the west wall of the first. Its unique feature is a series of casemates, square rooms abutting on the inner face of the wall. They were used as storerooms (huge storage jars—*dolia*—were found in them) and armories; their flat roofs could be used as fighting platforms. Outside the wall of the second citadel to the north-northwest is a large cistern, dimensions twenty by twenty-six feet, stone-built, lined with waterproof cement (*opus signinum*) and originally covered with a vault of limestone blocks. The excavators call the masonry technique Greek, and think the masons may have been brought from Histria, then under Dacian control. The technique is the same as at Costeşti, where nineteen Histrian coins prove trade relations. But the opus signinum and the vault are both Roman techniques; perhaps the cistern was built by the Roman engineers whom Decebalus cannily got from the Emperor Domitian as a part of the settlement after the war that ended in A.D. 89, in accordance with which the Dacian king, though technically he had lost the war, got a subsidy, recognition as an allied monarch, and the loan of skilled artisans.

Our third citadel, Piatra Roşie, lies 2,720 feet above sea level, and is more difficult of access than Costeşti or Blidaru, commanding another river valley to the west, two days' hike from Costeşti. Its name means "Red Rock": the stones of the plateau are the color of blood. Like Blidaru, it is a double fortress, built in two phases. The older part is a rectangular stone-walled enclosure measuring 148 by 345 feet—larger than a football field—equipped with towers (fig. 3.10). One entered through the tower in the upper left corner,

3.9. Blidaru, entrance

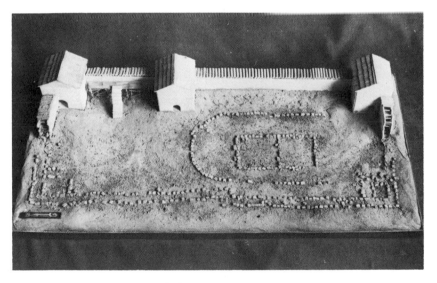

3.10. Piatra Roşie, model

thence up a flight of stone stairs, as carefully built as those leading to the royal tower house at Costeşti. Within, in the northern part of the open area to the right in the model, rose a rectangular wooden building, with forecourt and cella, like a temple, on stone footings. It had a beaten earth floor, a shingled or thatched roof, and a sturdy oak door with ornamental iron studs (now on display in the Museum of National History in Bucharest). Enclosing it on three sides was a stout U-shaped fence of wood plastered with clay mixed with straw and chaff, making a kind of crude stucco.

In its second phase, there was attached to the rectangular citadel, on the east, a larger area, almost square (442 by 492 feet), walled with rough stones and topped by a palisade. At its northeast and southeast corners were square stone towers that had been outpost watchtowers in the citadel's first phase. Within were traces of houses, on three terraces, and an apsidal building that looks like a temple, approached by a paved road.

Just north of the main citadel, Sarmizegethusa Regia, and visible from its steep rear approaches, lies Feţele Albe, 3,938 feet above sea level, where excavation was still going on in the summer of 1972.

3.11. Feţele Albe, plan

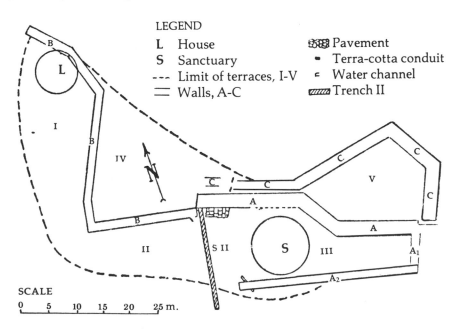

3.12. Grădiştea River

The remarkable feature of this site (fig. 3.11) is the series of retaining walls upholding five terraces: in an area measuring only 65 by 213 feet are more than 623 feet of retaining wall. On the various terraces are a round house with lower courses in limestone (fig. 3.11, L), a round sanctuary (fig. 3.11, S), houses with leveled clay floors, and a granary. Comparing small things with great, the excavators liken the terracing at Feţele Albe to that of the major Hellenistic city of Pergamum in Asia Minor.[3] The site yielded painted vases with human and animal figures, and a bronze casserole handle stamped with the name of an Italian manufacturer. The Romans destroyed the place in the First Dacian War; the inhabitants rebuilt it; the Romans subjected it to final destruction in A.D. 106, and built a castrum on the spot.

Sarmizegethusa Dacica, far the most impressive of the five citadels, lies at 3,937 feet, almost the same height above sea level as Feţele Albe. One reaches it in two stages; the round trip is an all-day journey. In the first stage, one mounts at 7:30 in the morning a little narrow-gauge lumber train that, on the days (Thursdays) when it delivers food and drink to the villagers along the line, takes six and a half hours to cover twelve miles. Passengers ride at the back of the train on a flatcar with wooden benches but no roof, which is inconvenient in wet weather. The line follows the west bank of the Grădiştea River, a brawling trout stream of great picturesqueness (fig. 3.12). On the east bank are the vestiges of the military road

3. MacKendrick, *Greek Stones Speak.* fig. 7.7.

that once served the needs of the Austrian army and perhaps of Trajan's legions. One leaves the little train at Cetate station and begins the second stage of the journey, a grueling climb, straight up, but well worth the effort, for the sanctuary and city of refuge on the high plateau of Sarmizegethusa, in the midst of a splendid forest of beech trees, constitute the most spectacular archaeological site in Romania and indeed are unique in all Europe.

The end of the steep path up the mountain to the Sarmizegethusa plateau is visible to the right of a sixty-columned sanctuary, like the ones at Costeşti, in the lower left quadrant of the model (fig. 3.13). This sanctuary was built in Burebista's time, and outmoded in Decebalus's by the more modern one, also of sixty columns, but larger; the drums are six and a half feet in diameter, eighteen inches wider than those in the old sanctuary (fig. 3.14). On the retaining wall between the new sanctuary and the terrace below (fig. 3.13, upper right quadrant), a series of Greek letters has been interpreted as a list of names, of gods, kings, or priests. On the lower terrace the Dacians built one square sanctuary, with eighteen columns (another multiple of six), and three round structures. The largest measures nearly one hundred feet across. It consists (fig. 3.15) of two concentric circles, with a horseshoe-shaped palisaded precinct within the inner one. The outer circle is made up of sets of six stone blocks interrupted by wider blocks, and repeated thirty times. It appears to represent six months of the Dacian solar year. The inner

3.13. Sarmizegethusa Regia, model

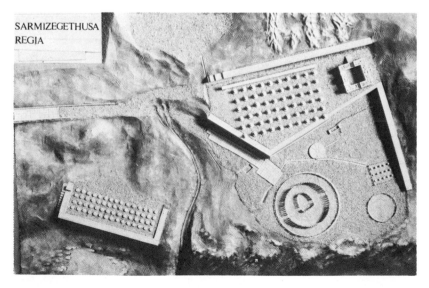

SARMIZEGETHUSA
REGIA

3.14. Sarmizegethusa Regia, old and new sanctuaries

3.15. Sarmizegethusa Regia, large round sanctuary

circle was a precinct marked off by wooden posts revetted with
polished and decorated terra-cotta plaques, with four entrances
marked by stone sills. This round precinct surrounded the innermost
horseshoe-shaped shrine. The smaller round sanctuary, forty feet
wide, to the east, is bounded by eleven sets of stone markers, in
groups of 8 + 1, one of 7 + 1, and one of 6 + 1. To the north of
the large round sanctuary is a stone disk twenty-three feet wide,
made up of ten pie-shaped wedges (fig. 3.16); it no doubt represents the sun.

West of the sacred area a paved road (fig. 3.17) leads through the
forest to the city of refuge, an irregular rectangle nearly seven and a
half acres in extent, impressively walled, with six levels of terraces.
In it the excavators found traces of log cabins on stone footings, with
handsome iron-studded doors, the walls faced with polished and
painted clay. The site yielded two important finds. One was a
medical kit, contained in a brassbound wooden box with an iron
handle. It contained a scalpel, tweezers, powdered pumice (apparently used, like kaolin, as an internal absorbent), and miniature
pots for pharmaceuticals. Here is evidence for empirical medicine,
practiced by a foreigner: the kit probably came from Italy. The other
important find was a huge vase, shaped like a champagne glass without a foot, twenty-four inches high and forty-one inches across. It is
stamped in mirror-writing, in the Roman alphabet, DECEBAL PER
SCORILO (fig. 3.18); i.e., Decebalus, son (*puer* in Latin) of Scorilus.
Scorilus, Decebalus's father and predecessor in the kingship, was one

3.16. Sarmizegethusa Regia, solar disk

3.17. Sarmizegethusa Regia, paved road

3.18. Sarmizegethusa Regia, *Decebal per Scorilo* vase, detail

of several shadowy figures who ruled over the remnants of the
Dacian state between Burebista's death in 44 B.C. and Decebalus's
accession in A.D. 87.[4] The site also yielded over four hundred iron
tools, made with the meter-long tongs, hammers, and anvils found
in the smithies north of the sanctuary: scythes, sickles, hoes, rakes,
picks, pruning hooks, knives, and plowshares. The excavators found
carpenters' tools, too: axes, chisels, adzes, saws, planes, and augers,
often in deposits, for shipment, or hidden, in dangerous times. Mis-
cellaneous ironmongery included spurs, crampons—for climbing the
mountain in winter—keys, barrel hoops, wagon parts, nails, spikes,
clamps, and hinges. There were weapons as well: daggers, curved
Dacian scimitars, spearpoints, shield-bosses. The Romans partly dis-
mantled the walls at the end of the First Dacian War in A.D. 102.
The Dacians rebuilt them. The Romans systematically destroyed
them in 106, and deported the inhabitants. As we shall see in the
next chapter, the reliefs on Trajan's Column in Rome tell the sad
story. On the plateau itself, calcined seeds tell the tale of the destruction of crops: wheat, millet, rye, barley, bedstraw, darnel, beans,
lentils, rape, spinach, mustard, and some odd ones, like hibiscus and
poppy, which conjure up images of flower gardens to relieve the
stark gray of the stone walls.

The Romans destroyed Decebalus's state just as it was coming to
full flower. The excavations in the Munţii Orăştiei area have thrown
new light on the political, economic, and scientific apogee of Dacian
culture, the latter testified to by the solar calendar. Burebista and
Decebalus creatively assimilated the technological achievements of
Greek and Roman culture, out of which Decebalus was in the process
of making a Dacian classical age when Trajan's legions struck the
final blow. Ironically, this assimilation was to facilitate the Romaniz-
ing of Dacia in the next century.

Recent excavation of the environs of the heartland citadels has
turned up some other sites, of greater or less importance; for ex-

---

4. Recently Kurt Horedt of Cluj has suggested that the inscription is Latin,
not Dacian, and that it is a potter's stamp: "From Decebalus's kiln, through the
agency of Scorilo." If this were so, the vessel would tell us nothing about
Decebalus's filiation, but it is hard to find an analogous potter's stamp in the
published collections.

ample, a series of conical brushwood huts, burned by the Romans in the Dacian wars, which must have sheltered shepherds pasturing their flocks in the foothills in the summer. Such huts were still to be seen in the remoter parts of Romania in the early years of this century; they are represented also on Trajan's Column.

Teams of archaeologists from Cluj, Deva, Sibiu, and Alba Iulia have also excavated four minor Dacian sites. The first is Căpîlna, built in an oak forest 2,000 feet above sea level, some twenty-five miles northeast of Sarmizegethusa. It has a stone-built murus Dacicus, originally fifteen feet high, with towers and a brick superstructure, roofed with oak. The masons who worked on the wall must have been more or less literate in Latin, for the marks on the blocks are in Roman letters. Finds of Roman coins range in date from 14 B.C. to A.D. 96–98—from Augustus to Trajan's predecessor Nerva. The citadel must have been the seat of a Dacian noble. Finds of agricultural tools show that his retainers were farmers; finds of jewelry—rings, bracelets, and fibulas in bronze and silver—show that they were prosperous enough to deck their wives in finery. But their prosperity ended when Trajan's legions burned their shingle-roofed wooden houses and their stores of grain in the Second Dacian War.

The southernmost Transylvanian fortress so far found is Bănița, perched in a beech forest 2,966 feet above sea level, some fifteen miles southeast of Sarmizegethusa (fig. 4.1). It, too, had its murus Dacicus, its fighting platforms, its towers, and its earthwork, its stairs and terraces, its pitched-roofed, shingled wooden houses, and its columned sanctuary. There was of course plenty of timber, and a quarry on the spot. Finds of crucibles, and molds for casting metal, testify to the activity of its craftsmen. The clever adaptation of its buildings to the terrain illustrates, here as elsewhere, the truth of a remark by a Roman author, "Daci inhaerent montibus"—the Dacians cling like limpets to their mountains. Bănița was intended to guard Decebalus's capital from invasion from the south, but it, too, went up in flames in the Great War.

A third site, Tilișca, is beautifully located in a pine forest above a clear stream, 2,330 feet above sea level, a dozen miles southeast of Căpîlna. Its discovery came about accidentally, the result of noticing some blocks built into the foundations of a modern house in the village below. The blocks must have come from a Dacian citadel,

3.19. Tilişca, coining dies

since they bore the characteristic cuttings for inserting the crossbeams of a murus Dacicus. The citadel itself proved to be of the usual type, with earthwork, stone wall, gate, towers, cistern, house foundations, and evidence of burning by the Romans. What is unusual about Tilişca is the discovery of a workshop where coins were minted. The coiner's kit (fig. 3.19) had been hidden in a clay pot. It consisted of fourteen bronze punch-dies—of which the photograph shows ten—and three iron anvil-dies. The ancient coiner put a silver disk, or flan, between the two dies, hit the punch die with a hammer, and thus struck his coin. The devices on the disks are those of Roman silver denarii, dated between 145–138 and 72 B.C. There can be little doubt that our Tilişca workman was a counterfeiter.

The fourth and last minor Transylvanian site deserving notice here is Piatra Craivii (fig. 4.1), 3,544 feet above sea level, in the mountains twelve miles north of Alba Iulia, ancient Apulum, itself a Dacian site that was to acquire greater importance as a center of Roman provincial government (see chapter 5). Piatra Craivii has all the Dacian hallmarks, including a sanctuary with thirty (five times six) columns. What makes it worthy of notice is its function: it was used to guard the approaches to the gold mines in the Apuseni Mountains to the northwest. The gold was an important source of revenue to the Dacian kings, who probably held the mines as a monopoly. To acquire the monopoly for themselves was a major motive, to the Romans, for their invasion; the emperors, as we shall see, held the monopoly in their own hands for the 165 years of the Roman occupation.

It remains to discuss briefly the evidence for four Dacian settlements in the mountainous northeastern region, Moldavia. The first is Bîtca Doamnei (fig. 1.1, no. 28), sited on a terraced seven-and-a-half-acre plateau 460 feet above the Bistriţa River, two and a half miles west of Piatra Neamţ. The hand of man has wrought great havoc here; the destructive forces include a Tatar invasion in the thirteenth century, military installations in World Wars I and II, and indiscriminate treasure hunting. Only in the planting of conifers have the ancient levels been disturbed in a good cause. But patient and careful excavation has brought to light a palisaded earthwork eleven and a half feet thick. The palisade consisted of wooden uprights with planks nailed horizontally to both their inner and their outer faces, the space between filled with clay and small stones. Outside the palisade is a triple ditch of uncertain ·date; on the inside, a guard walk ran between the palisade and the stone wall. This inner stone wall was perhaps originally thirteen to sixteen feet high, with towers built of stone in their lower courses, sun-dried brick above. Their height—twenty-three feet—was calculated by observing how far from the wall the bricks of the upper courses fell.

One entered the settlement through a wooden gate eight feet wide. The houses appear to have been half-timbered, on stone foundations; they had packed clay floors and whitewashed interior walls. Their doors, of wood, were iron-braced, or ornamentally studded, as at Sarmizegethusa. The roofs were shingled. Since few nails were found, the assumption is that wooden pegs held the houses together. One house with multiple rooms has been dignified by the name of "palace," but its construction is nowhere nearly so sophisticated as that of the tower house at Costeşti. The discovery of a kiln and fragments of slag suggests that artisans—potters and metalworkers— lived together in a craftsman's quarter. The potters produced some imitations of both Greek and Roman ware. The metalworkers made plowshares, sickles, anvils, chisels, adzes, gimlets, shears and knives, clamps, spikes, and rivets. The output of arms was not large: the Romans found this unwarlike people easy prey. Two columned sanctuaries were found, one just outside the wall to the south, the other just inside, with a defense tower built over it. When the gods were on the side of the bigger battalions, obviously something had to.give. Finds of jewelry evince a modest prosperity: fibulas in iron, bronze, and gold; bronze rings, and one in gold, with snake-headed finials; a bronze bracelet. The only two coins found show trade relations with the West: a silver coin of Dyrrhachium (second century B.C.), and a Roman denarius of 91 B.C. The close general resemblance to Transylvanian sites warrants the inference that Bîtca Doamnei was a part of Burebista's and Decebalus's kingdom.

Just north of Piatra Neamţ, and within eyeshot of Bîtca Doamnei, the Dacian site of Cozla (fig. 1.1, no. 29), now a national park, shows the usual features. It also ended in destruction by fire. So did Tiseşti (Tg. Ocna on the map, fig. 3.1), forty-five miles to the south.

The last site, Bărboşi, near Galaţi, not far from the confluence of the Danube and the Siret, is better known as the seat of a Roman camp. But there are Dacian levels below. The settlement was palisaded (the region has no stone). Within the palisade were wattle-and-daub houses with tile roofs after the Greek fashion: Bărboşi is only some sixty miles northwest of Histria. There was a columned sanctuary: the column drums, *faute de mieux,* were made of wood. There were many Greek imports among the pottery. While many of the coins were of Histria and Tomis, Roman Republican denarii show that trade also came from the other way, as did Dacian Bărboşi's final destruction. The Romans may well have felt justified in wreaking vengeance on the place, for from it must have been launched many of the barbarian raids described by the Roman poet Ovid, in exile at Tomis in the early years of the Christian era. Ovid depicts the natives crossing the frozen Danube in the winter on the ice, their archers firing their poisoned arrows within the very walls of the city.

The Dacian state whose citadels and settlements we have been describing in this chapter might, left to itself, have developed a culture worthy of comparison with Rome's. But greed and violence on both sides prevented peaceful development. The Dacians acquired a taste for Roman luxury goods and raided Roman territory as a convenient source of the means to buy them. The Romans wanted Dacian gold, and burned to avenge their raided towns. How matters came to a head early in the reign of Trajan—the emperor called, by the Romans, Optimus Princeps, "the best of princes"—will be the subject of the next chapter.

4. THE ROMAN CONQUEST

A Column and a Trophy

Official historians are ever ready to record that their nation never fought an unjust war, and Roman historians are no exception to the rule. The official motive for Trajan's Dacian campaigns of A.D. 101–2 and 105–6 was to wipe out the disgrace of Domitian's peace of 89, after a war significant enough to have tempted the pen of the historian Cornelius Tacitus, in a work now lost. It was alleged, no doubt with truth, that Decebalus had received deserters, and paid Roman money, given him to keep the peace, to Roman engineers to build strongholds for him against the Romans. But there was unquestionably also an economic motive in the lure of the Dacian gold mines. Dacia had a reputation for fabulous wealth, much like an El Dorado or a California. But, whatever the motives, the Roman aggression, if successful, meant death to the Dacian state, and so the resistance was heroic. Fortunately for us, both the aggression and the heroism are visually and strikingly recorded on two remarkable surviving monuments: the sculptured scroll of Trajan's Column in Rome and the metopes and crenellations of his trophy at Adamclisi in Dobruja (fig. 2.1). These we shall use, with all due caution, as our chief sources for the description in this chapter of Trajan's two Dacian wars.

Trajan's preparations took three years. He had to assemble a force of Roman legionaries and non-Roman auxiliaries (cavalry, bowmen, slingers), all represented on the column, and estimated at 100,000 to 150,000 men. He had to make elaborate logistic preparations, especially in the matter of building military roads. In the summer of 1971 there was still visible on the Yugoslav bank of the Danube, opposite Ogradena (fig. 1.1, no. 33), six miles southwest of Orșova (ancient Dierna; fig. 4.1), an inscription, the Tabula Traiana, carved

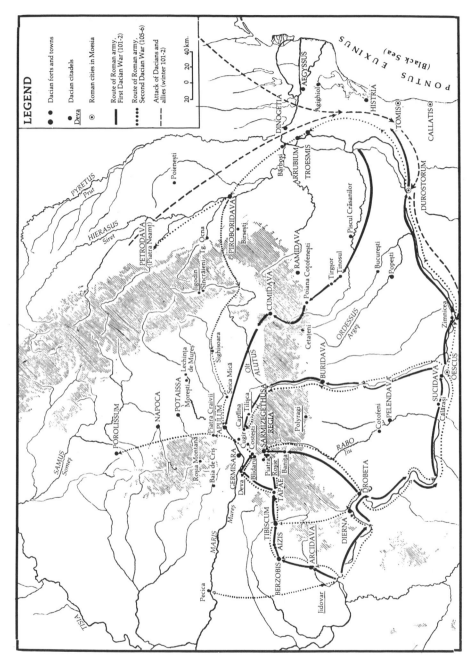

4.1. Trajan's Dacian Wars, map

in the living rock, recording how Trajan cut away mountains and removed projecting spurs of stone to build a road under the cliffs along
the river bank, a remarkable feat of engineering. The construction
of the new hydroelectric dam at the Iron Gates bids fair to change
the water level and inundate both road and inscription.

At last, on March 25, A.D. 101, all was ready. We happen to know
the exact date because the priests in Rome—the prestigious Arval
Brethren—who offered the prayer at Trajan's departure recorded it
on stone, and the inscription survives in the courtyard of Rome's
Terme Museum. In Rome's Capitoline Temple the priests prayed to
Jupiter the Best and Greatest for the speedy victory and safe return
of Trajan (the Best of Princes) named with his rank and titles; they
promised the sacrifice of a bull with gilded horns if their prayer was
granted. That they made the same prayer and promise to eleven
other gods, goddesses, and personified abstractions—including Mars,
god of war, Neptune the Guardian of Voyagers by Sea and River,
Hercules the Performer of Labors, and Fortuna Redux (Lady Luck
Who Giveth Safe Return)—suggests the importance attached to the
expedition and the difficulties foreseen before its successful out-
come.

Trajan himself kept a campaign journal, of which all is lost save a
single sentence. But the journal must have served as the main factual
basis for the record carved on the column, which must now be described. Dedicated on May 12, A.D. 113, it was at least seven years in
the making, and no wonder, for it stands 130 feet high, with seven-
teen superimposed marble drums, each twelve feet in diameter, on
which was carved, after the shaft was erected, a marble scroll in a
spiral 656 feet long, containing 155 separate scenes and over twenty-
five hundred figures. It is Trajan's monument in a double sense, for
after his death his ashes were collected in a golden urn and deposited
in a room in the base of the column. The gilt bronze statue of the
emperor that once surmounted the column was replaced in 1588 by
the present statue of St. Peter. One may by special permission climb
the 185-step spiral stair to the top of the column, but this of course
gives no view of the reliefs. These in antiquity could best be seen
from the porch-roofs of the libraries that flanked the column. Yet a
consecutive appreciation of the narrative would require the viewer to
go round and round the column like a horse in a circus ring. It is as

hard to view as the Sistine Chapel ceiling, and as rewarding. During World War II, when it was protected against air raids by scaffolding, direct head-on close-up photographs were taken of the reliefs, but these were not well reproduced; the photographs presented here come from casts. The casts themselves can most conveniently be seen in the Victoria and Albert Museum in London; in the Museo della Civiltà Romana in the grounds of the Esposizione Universale Romana, south of Rome; or in the new Museum of National History in Bucharest.

So ambitious a project could not physically have been the work of one man, and indeed the artistic quality of the reliefs varies with the competence of the master or apprentice who worked on a given section. But the overall plan was the work of a sculptor of genius. He knew how to make the relief just high enough to stand out without breaking the architectonic line of the shaft; his figures are energetic, his composition balanced; he contrives to maintain a tension between rhetorical tone and historical narrative; he is extremely skilled in his use of contrast and in manipulating the space at his disposal; above all, he shows a humane understanding of and compassion for the plight of the conquered. For the reliefs are not merely a Battle Hymn of the Republic, or even simply an evocation of the blood, sweat, and tears which are the price of warfare for both victors and vanquished. Scenes of combat do not predominate: battles take up only a quarter of the total space. The overriding theme is the might and majesty of the Roman Peace. Naturally, Trajan is omnipresent, but he is so not merely as a conqueror, but as a paragon of clemency, justice, and piety—the king-becoming graces. Yet the hero of the reliefs is not he, but the anonymous, hard-working, foot-slogging, disciplined Roman soldier. And the heroism of the Dacians in adversity, the dignity of Decebalus in defeat, are portrayed with a humanism that reflects the greatest credit on the anonymous sculptor who created this masterpiece. Some scholars would remove the anonymity, supposing that the design and execution of the column reliefs should be ascribed to Trajan's Syrian architect, Apollodorus of Damascus, from whose planning-board came Trajan's Forum, of which the column was an important part, and the famous bridge across the Danube, to be described below.

In the absence of contemporary literary sources about Trajan's

Dacian wars, it would be folly to take the column reliefs as verbatim evidence for details of the campaigns. The sculptor and his apprentices had almost certainly never been on the scene in Dacia; besides, however much the master planner may have sympathized with the underdog, he could hardly be expected to show Roman arms worsted: among all the twenty-five hundred figures a wounded Roman soldier is shown only once.

Students of the column have run a gamut of assessments of its trustworthiness as a historical source. At one extreme are those literalists who take it as an accurate topographical map of the campaigns; at the other, the art-history aesthetes who argue that it is not true to historical fact, but follows closely the rhetorical artistic conventions of paintings and sculptures regularly carried in Roman triumphal processions. The truth, as often, lies somewhere between the extremes. We can illustrate this by considering the six themes that recur most often: (1) addresses by Trajan to his troops; (2) religious sacrifices upon emergent occasions; (3) building operations; (4) Trajan's receiving ambassadors and prisoners; (5) the army on the march; and (6) landscape and architecture. Of these, (1) and (2) are admittedly artistic conventions, but in the address-scenes Trajan is a recognizable portrait, and perhaps so is his lieutenant and successor Hadrian, as well as Licinius Sura, the Spaniard who was Trajan's frontier expert, friend, and ghost-writer.[1] The sacrifices are true to Roman religious ritual, with all the right animals (ox, boar, sheep), priests, and attendants. The building operations, in which over two hundred people participate, must be true to the facts of the campaigns, which involved much military engineering: building of camps, roads, bridges, and pontoons, dismantling of captured enemy fortifications. But, as we shall see, any attempt to identify localities with absolute precision is impossible. The embassies and prisoners could be taken from life, from Dacians present in Rome. Their dress (trousers), hair, and beards are accurately rendered, and Decebalus is a recognizable portrait. Scenes of the army on the march are conventional in that they are planned to fit the space: eleven in twenty-two spirals. And they permit us to identify locales only in the

1. See Paul MacKendrick, *The Iberian Stones Speak* (New York, 1967), p. 162.

most general way. Finally, the details of landscape and architecture were entrusted to apprentices, and precise identification of places is difficult or controversial. Roman camps that were in fact earthworks are shown as stone-built and the details of Dacian construction methods are untrustworthy, while the absence of any representation of the characteristic rectangular or round columned sanctuaries gives ground for mistrust.

Yet for a knowledge of Trajan's Dacian wars, the column is essentially all we have, and it is surprising how much it can be induced to tell us if we do not press the evidence too hard. The strict chronological order of speeches, sacrifices, councils of war, building of camps, marches, and battles must be right, since the reliefs represent contemporary history, and surviving participants would be quick to spot gross inaccuracies. Though the column has been compared to a film not shot on location, the general topography and direction of march can, with a little good will, be made out in most cases, especially with the help of what the excavations of a generation of dedicated Romanian archaeologists can now tell us.

In what follows, I shall use the Roman numerals of Cichorius (see bibliography) to identify the reliefs. Scenes I and II begin with Danubian frontier posts, palisaded, with balconies supplied with torches for signaling at night, very like those on the German frontier.[2] They also have woodpiles and haystacks for thatching and fodder. We see barrels of provisions being offloaded on the Roman (south) bank of the Danube. Scene III shows a stronghold walled with squared blocks, probably Viminacium (Kostolač, Yugoslavia; fig. 5.1), where the Romans had had an outpost for over fifty years. Opposite it on the Romanian bank was Lederata, from which a road led northward to Arcidava (now Vărădia, site of a forty-acre Roman legionary camp; fig. 4.1), and Berzobis, then east via Aizis to Tibiscum. The sole surviving sentence from Trajan's campaign journal records the Berzobis-Aizis leg of his journey. At Berzobis (now Reşiţa) a fifty-acre Trajanic camp has been excavated, large enough to hold a legion; one of the finds was a legionary helmet (fig. 4.2).

Trajan's legions split into two prongs, and converged on Tibiscum. The second detachment started from either Dierna (Orşova) or Drobeta (Turnu Severin), crossing from the south bank of the

2. See MacKendrick, *Romans on the Rhine,* figs. 4.2 and 4.10.

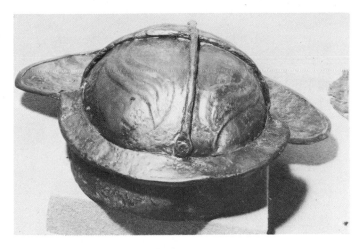

4.2. Berzobis, Roman helmet

Danube on a pontoon bridge represented on the column (scene IV), where we see the legions behind their standards, in full marching kit, helmets slung over shoulder, heavy pack on back, with Trajan leading the Praetorian Guard. The next scenes portray a council of war and a sacrifice. Present is a barbarian (scene VII: fig. 4.3) who has fallen off his mule, perhaps in wonder at the noise made by the legionary bandsmen tootling above his head. Tied to his mule's saddle is a round, perforated object, which may well be the mushroom on which, according to Dio Cassius, Trajan's barbarian allies wrote a message advising him to turn back and keep the peace.

4.3. Trajan's Column, mushroom message

4.4. Trajan's Column, Dacian prisoner

4.5. Trajan's Column, severed heads

4.6. Trajan's Column, Costeşti

Succeeding scenes show Trajan making speeches, the legionaries building camps and roads, and Trajan receiving a Dacian prisoner, brought in by auxiliaries, who are pulling him by the hair and holding his arm in a hammerlock (scene XVIII: fig. 4.4). After further scenes of bridge- and camp-building, scene XXIII (fig. 4.5) shows a major battle, probably at Tapae, the "Iron Gates of Transylvania": a pair of auxiliaries offer severed Dacian heads to Trajan, who is revolted. Jupiter with his thunderbolt protects the bigger battalions. A young Dacian, wounded or dead, droops pathetically in his comrades' arms; above, Decebalus and Trajan survey the carnage (fig. 4.6). To the right we see Trajan before a Dacian fortress, its battlements adorned with the impaled heads of Roman soldiers. The Dacians were keen for the fray. The Greek rhetorician Dio Chrysostom, who may have visited the Dacian capital about this time, describes them as impatient of speeches, high-strung, tense as racehorses; everywhere arms and chargers, as strong men marshaled their power to fight for freedom. The houses on stilts within the wall suggest that the fortress is Costeşti, where, as we saw, excavation revealed such structures. In front of the walls are "tank-traps,"[3] the use of which Decebalus will have learned from the Roman engineers supplied by Domitian. In the foreground, Roman soldiers are setting fire to Dacian wooden, shingle-roofed tower houses outside the walls. The Dacians retreat, the Romans carry on, Trajan makes a speech, and the first campaign ends with the reception of Dacian ambassadors, mopping-up operations, houses being set afire, families fleeing, live-stock (oxen, sheep, a donkey) lying dead.

Scenes XXXI-XLVII portray Trajan's reaction to a change in tactics by Decebalus, who moved rapidly east to attack Roman strong-holds in Dobruja, now the Roman province of Moesia Inferior. We see the Dacian host, with their dragon standards and scale-armored mounted allies (fig. 4.7) crossing the turbulent Danube and attack-ing a Roman fortress with a battering ram—another technique learned from Domitian's Roman engineers. Trajan embarks in pur-suit, himself taking the flagship's helm. By forced marches he arrives at the scene of a night battle (XXXVIII); in the background are Dacian wagons; over the wheel of one hangs the mutilated body of a child. The wagons reoccur on some of the metopes of the Tro-paeum Traiani at Adamclisi; Adamclisi may be the scene of the battle on the column. Particularly fearsome are the Roman native auxiliaries, half-naked, and armed with nail-studded clubs. These Dacians submit, but another major battle presents the picture (scene XL: fig. 4.8) of the sole wounded Roman soldier on the column. But the Romans win this battle, too. Some Dacians flee, others are taken prisoner. Trajan distributes money to the auxiliaries, who kiss his hand. In a strongly contrasting scene (XLV: fig. 4.9), Dacian women torture naked Roman prisoners, beating them, pulling their hair, and burning their flesh with torches. But the Romans have won: Trajan reembarks upriver, the troops offload baggage, and the Dobruja campaign is over.

The third and last campaign of the First Dacian War begins with infantry, cavalry, and wagon train on the march northward from the Danube to Decebalus's capital, perhaps via Bumbești (see map, fig. 5.1)—where a Trajanic earthwork has been discovered—and the Vîlcan Pass. Trajan receives a Dacian embassy, performs sacrifice, and presses onward, the army road-building as it goes. In one scene

3. See Paul MacKendrick, *Roman France* (New York, 1972), fig. 2.6.

4.7. Trajan's Column, scale armor

(LVI) the work is proceeding in front of a camp with impaled
Dacian heads displayed before it. Roman cavalrymen seize and burn
a palisaded Dacian camp. Some Dacians retreat; others kneel before
Trajan in entreaty. But he marches implacably on: we see Moorish
cavalry (scene LXIV), their hair in ringlets, making punitive raids,
riding bareback on Arabian horses. In a major battle (scene LXVI),
perhaps fought at Petroşeni (fig. 1.1, no. 36), at the north end of
the Vîlcan Pass, artillery is brought to bear: we see mule-drawn
catapult wagons, catapults mounted on the camp walls, wooden platforms for catapults. Decebalus has trouble with deserters: a Dacian

4.8. Trajan's Column, wounded Roman

4.9. Trajan's Column, Dacian women torture Roman prisoner

4.10. Trajan's Column, Balearic slingers

nobleman, identified by his characteristic cap, has turned Quisling, and kisses Trajan's hand. Another nobleman, more loyal to the Dacian cause, is taken prisoner. Under the tortoise-like protection of their locked shields, Roman soldiers storm a Dacian citadel, fighting their way up a flight of steps, like those discovered at Costeşti or Piatra Roşie. The sculptor's apprentice has made a botched attempt to render a murus Dacicus, with wooden beam-ends projecting between stone courses.

The last battle of the first war (scene LXXII) is a hand-to-hand mêlée. Trajan again rejects with distaste the severed heads of two Dacians, offered to him by two auxiliaries, identifiable by uniforms and shield. Balearic slingers (fig. 4.10) are brought into play: they carry spare bullets in a fold of their tunics and wear a spare sling as a headband; in the heat of the battle they trample on the Dacian dead and wounded. Most of the Dacians abase themselves before Trajan; high on a cliff behind them stands an aloof and noble figure (fig. 4.11). It is Decebalus. He had to surrender on harsh terms, recorded by Dio: disarmament, the handing over of Roman deserters

4.11. Trajan's Column, Decebalus

and technicians, the tearing down of his walls, withdrawal from captured territory, and the renunciation of any independent foreign policy. In scene LXXVI (fig. 4.12), the Dacians withdraw, with their families, flocks, and herds. Mothers hold babies in their arms, or carry them in a cradle on their heads; fathers carry their sons on their shoulders, or drag an unwilling youngster by the arm. We see a group of Dacians, in keeping with the peace terms, dismantling their own walls, while above them a pair whispers together, perhaps conspiring to defy the terms. Trajan, in travel dress, makes a farewell speech to the army of occupation. Ending the reliefs of the first war, a winged Victory, flanked by trophies, inscribes a shield, perhaps with Trajan's virtues: courage, clemency, justice, and piety.

4.12. Trajan's Column, Dacian withdrawal

Decebalus having violated all the terms of the treaty, Trajan de-
clared war on him a second time, and set out from Rome on June 4,
A.D. 105: again the inscribed prayers of the Arval Brethren (this
time with an assist from the *Fasti Ostienses*) supply the precise date.
The early scenes of the Second Dacian War need not concern us,
since they do not involve Dacia. Trajan embarks from an Adriatic
port, lands somewhere in Dalmatia, and proceeds across country to
the Danube, greeted en route by deputations and religious sacrifices
in his honor. Scene XCIX (fig. 4.13), the most famous on the
column, shows him arrived and offering sacrifice at Drobeta, where
Apollodorus of Damascus has just finished his famous bridge. The
sculptor shows the stone piers, wooden superstructure, and monumental arch at the north end; the model (fig. 4.14), in the Iron
Gates Museum at Turnu Severin, gives clearer detail, of cutwaters,

4.13. Trajan's Column, Drobeta bridge

4.14. Drobeta bridge, model

trusses, triple concentric arches between the piers, balustrade, and monumental gate. There was a corresponding gate at the south end. It, like its Romanian fellow, was surmounted by statuary. A fine bronze head, fished out of the river at the south gate in 1850, and now in the Belgrade museum, formed part of this decoration: it may represent Trajan's father, or Claudius Livianus, prefect of his Praetorian Guard. Of the excavated bridgehead camp at Drobeta the modern visitor can see one of the great north piers, beside the railway line on which travels a crack train called Traian. At low water, swirls in the Danube show the location of other piers. The Iron Gates Museum displays blocks from the piers, and massive oak beams from the caissons and/or the superstructure. Many of the piers were destroyed in the last century as hindrances to navigation. Dio is lost in admiration at the magnitude, difficulty, and expense of the bridge-building operation. The bridge, nearly 4,000 feet long, had twenty piers of squared stone laid without mortar; they had to be constructed in caissons. The piers rose 150 feet from their footings in the muddy riverbed; they were 60 Roman feet wide, and the span of each arch was 170 Roman feet. The top blocks of the piers were scored for the seating of the wooden superstructure. Trajan's successor, Hadrian, removed the superstructure, to deny the bridge to raiding barbarians. But in Dio's time (ca. A.D. 230), the stone piers still stood, "as if they had been erected solely to show that there is nothing which human ingenuity cannot accomplish."

At Drobeta, the column shows Trajan receiving eight different embassies, distinguished by their dress or hair style: Scythians in mittens, Germans with their hair in a knot, Greeks in dignified long robes, wearing headbands; Iazyges from Pannonia (modern Hungary) in sugarloaf hats, and carrying quivers.

The Romans press on into the mountains, greet Trajan, perform sacrifice: Trajan makes a speech, holds a council of war, and presses on toward Decebalus's capital. The legionaries live off the country; scene CIX (fig. 4.15) shows them unafraid (without helmets), cutting wheat—it is high summer of A.D. 106—in front of a walled camp with tents.

The Romans storm the Dacian capital, which is reduced to desperate straits: scene CXX (fig. 4.16) has been variously interpreted as a mass suicide, or the sharing of the last ration of water in the

4.15. Trajan's Column, foraging

beleaguered citadel. The lower right corner shows a Dacian already in his grave. A detail (fig. 4.17) reveals the pathos and humanity of which the sculptor is capable: a Dacian, mourning his dead son, wipes his eyes with a corner of his tunic. Some Dacians flee; others submit. The Romans take and loot the capital; the army acclaims the victorious Trajan.

But pockets of resistance still hold out; the Roman army marches north, farther into Transylvania. A traitor betrays the hiding place of Decebalus's treasure, which the king had diverted a river to conceal; scene CXXXVIII (fig. 4.18) shows it being loaded onto horses or mules for transport to Rome. Some Dacians decide to flee, others commit suicide, still others try to buy amnesty: one offers to Trajan a tray of three gold ingots. Decebalus, "unconquerable except by death, which does not count in honor" (the words are Winston Churchill's), commits suicide (scene CXLV: fig. 4.19), slitting his throat with his curved Dacian dagger. His head and right hand are displayed to the army, and later taken to Rome to grace—if that is the right word—Trajan's triumph. Recently a young American scholar discovered in the Cavala museum, in northern Greece, the tombstone of the soldier who brought Decebalus's head to Trajan.

The Romans inexorably rout out, surround, attack, and seize the Dacian remnant. One of the last scenes on the column (CXLIX: fig. 4.20) shows the survivors, in a mountain landscape, the haunt of boar and stag, setting off into exile, as the spiral narrows, with what is left of their flocks and herds, to a new and humbler life as Roman subjects. The last carving on the column represents—is it symbolic?—a stunted tree.

By early August, A.D. 106, the war was over, and Dacia was constituted a Roman province. Trajan celebrated a triumph, gave 123 days of games—with unprecedented slaughter of wild animals in beast-fights in the arena—and with the spoils of Dacia built his forum and his column. Dacian losses were heavy: prisoners alone numbered fifty thousand. But Dacian life was not stunted: it lived on through the 165 years of Roman occupation. Romanization let Dacians prosper, without losing their indigenous culture, and when the Romans withdrew in A.D. 271, the Dacians carried on, profiting from what they had learned from their Roman masters, speaking the Latin that is still the root of the Romanian language, and fully conscious of their cultural heritage from Rome, which lives on in the Romanian cultural commitment to the West.

4.16. Trajan's Column, water-sharing or suicide

4.17. Trajan's Column, mourning Dacian

4.18. Trajan's Column, booty

4.19. Trajan's Column, Decebalus's suicide

4.20. Trajan's Column, final Dacian withdrawal

4.21. Adamclisi,
trophy and model

Trajan's Column in Rome is a familiar memorial of his Dacian wars. His trophy at Adamclisi in Dobruja is, undeservedly, not so well known. Its forty-nine surviving sculptured metopes form the most remarkable monument of primitive provincial art in the Roman world. Trajan commissioned it either to celebrate a major victory in his First Dacian War (column, scene XXXVIII), or to commemorate some of the fallen in Domitian's war of A.D. 85–89,[4] or for both reasons. It is a huge limestone-faced concrete drum, one hundred feet in diameter, standing, visible from miles away, on a bare, windswept hill forty miles southwest of Constanţa, and eleven miles south of the Danube.

The drum (fig. 4.21), stood on a nine-stepped platform. It was faced with seven courses of dressed stone; the sculptured metopes, averaging five feet high by four feet wide, originally fifty-four in number, framed by ornamental friezes, ran either halfway up, or under the cornice. Above the cornice ran a parapet, with geometric motifs, lion waterspouts, and twenty-six crenellations, each sculptured with the figure of a trousered prisoner, his hands tied behind his back, standing beside a tree. The prisoner in figure 4.22 is identified as a German from the lateral knot in his hair. Dacians and Sarmatians are also represented. Behind the parapet rose the conical roof, covered with U-shaped marble tiles. From the apex of the cone rose a two-story hexagonal pedestal, bearing two identical inscriptions dating the monument in A.D. 109, and dedicating it to Mars the Avenger—which is one reason why some scholars suppose that Trajan meant it to commemorate the dead in Domitian's war. Others argue that Mars the Avenger was in general the patron saint of the Roman army, and that the monument has nothing to do with Domitian's war. On the pedestal rose the trophy itself, nearly 33 feet high, with three captives at its feet. This brings the total height of the monument to 130 feet, the same as Trajan's Column in

---

4. This hypothesis depends on attributing to Domitian's war an altar several hundred meters east of the trophy, inscribed to the memory of "the heroes who, dying for their country, fell in the Dacian War," and recording thirty-eight hundred names. Many scholars find this attribution impossible, and assign the altar to Trajan's war. Similarly, it is controversial whether the remains of a huge mausoleum, northeast of the altar, commemorate a Domitianic or a Trajanic general. Excavations in 1971 found nothing to solve the problem.

4.22. Adamclisi trophy, German prisoner

Rome. The impressive fragments of the trophy are now displayed at the foot of the drum, together with the metopes, protected by glass, in a circle of the same diameter as the drum. On the opposite side of the drum the sculptures of the parapet, also glass-enclosed, stand in a semicircle.

The original order of the metopes is controversial. That presented here is F. B. Florescu's of 1965, the one followed in the actual display of the metopes on the site. Florescu came to his conclusions on objective architectural grounds, having nothing to do with a priori notions about whether the metopes portray battles of the First Dacian War, or of both. (In fact, since there is no evidence that Trajan was in Dobruja in his second war, it is more likely that the metopes record only the campaign pictured in scenes XXXI-XLVII of the column.) Florescu's arrangement is based on close observation of the frames of the metopes. These consist of friezes at top and bottom, and pilasters on either side. The upper frieze has slots of varying length in its bottom surface, into which the tops of the metopes were designed to fit. The lower frieze has slots in its top surface, into which the pilasters were designed to fit. Since the metopes are of slightly varying width, and since nearly all the upper frieze blocks are preserved, the order of the metopes can be determined on purely mathematical grounds, with only a very small margin of error. A secondary determinant is the findspots of the metopes on the ground around the drum, where they were thrown by an earthquake. This is a secondary consideration because the findspots are variously reported. The third consideration is the subject matter of the metopes themselves. They portray hand-to-hand fighting between the Romans and the Dacians, plus their allies; one or more battles involving a Dacian wagon train (as on the column); the spoils of war; the presence of Trajan and his staff (as on the column); and Dacian prisoners, men, women, and children (again matched on the column).

Metopes XXI, XXXIV, and XXXVII (figs. 4.23–4.25) show scenes of hand-to-hand combat. In figure 4.23 a Roman soldier, in iron armor, with shield, helmet, and broadsword, attacks a bearded antagonist in a heavy woolen cloak, who wields a curved two-handed Sarmatian scimitar. On the ground, neatly folded to fit the corner of the metope, sits a trousered German (his hair in a lateral knot), eyes

4.23. Adamclisi trophy, hand-to-hand combat

closed in exhaustion, his weapon over his shoulder. As often on the column, the Roman treads unfeelingly on his victim's leg. In figure 4.24 a Roman legionary in chain mail attacks a naked Dacian archer in a tree. Another naked Dacian lies beheaded on the ground, his shield propped behind him. The sword is Roman, propped upright as a symbol of vengeance. In figure 4.25 another Roman in chain mail fends off two antagonists, naked to the waist: they are probably German allies of the Dacians. One brandishes his wicked two-handed scimitar, trying to undercut the Roman's shield; the other is poised for flight. Above hangs, apparently suspended in mid-air, a naked, bearded barbarian, distorted to fit the space. The same sort of figure is to be seen on the column.

From the scene of one of the battles near the Dacian wagon train comes metope XLII (fig. 4.26), portraying a Dacian family, father, mother, and child, in a four-wheeled ox-drawn wagon, their possessions in a locked box behind them. The wagoner, stripped to the waist, a staff on his shoulder, walks beside the ox, identified as such by his cloven hoofs.

The primitive vigor of the sculpture is nowhere better shown than in metope XLIV (fig. 4.27), with its splendid trio of sheep and pair of rampant goats, symbolizing, no doubt, the rich Dacian flocks that fell as spoils into the hands of the victorious Romans.

Metope XLIX (fig. 4.28) unmistakably shows Trajan (characteristic hair style, eagle emblem on breast), with a member of his staff. Radu Florescu's grouping of the fifty-four metopes, which challenges Bobu Florescu's, assumes six sets of nine, with Trajan as the central figure of each. Whatever the proper sequence, Roman victory is inevitable. Metope LI (fig. 4.29) shows a Roman officer between two Dacian prisoners, chained, with their arms bound behind their backs. Finally, metope LIV (fig. 4.30), a great favorite with modern Romanian patriots, shows the innocent victims of all warfare: two Dacian women; one holds in her arms a child wrapped in a fold of her garment.

4.24. Adamclisi trophy, hand-to-hand combat

4.25. Adamclisi trophy, hand-to-hand combat

4.26. Adamclisi trophy, Dacian family

4.27. Adamclisi trophy, booty, sheep and goats

4.28. Adamclisi trophy,
Trajan

4.29. Adamclisi trophy,
Roman officer
with prisoners

As a work of art, the trophy is inferior to the column: cruder in execution, narrower in scope. But both, it seems to me, convey the same message: Roman arms are invincible, but the Dacians' heroism is admirable, their lot pathetic. It was indeed a pity that Decebalus and his state were both cut down in their prime. But in Dacia, as elsewhere, the Romans contrived to consolidate by the arts of peace what they had won by the inexorability of war. The war was no sooner over than Trajan set about organizing Dacia as a province of the Roman Empire. How that organization worked, what Roman Dacia looked like, and to what extent the Dacians prospered under Roman rule will be the subject of the next chapter.

4.30. Adamclisi trophy, Dacian mother and child

5.1. Roman Dacia, map

5. DACIA UNDER
ROMAN RULE
A.D. 106−271

The 165-year history of Roman Dacia concerns a province that was a bastion of empire projecting like a huge thumb (fig. 5.1) into what the Romans regarded as barbarian country, on both sides of the new frontier. But, though they kept in the province an army of occupation estimated, at its height, at over fifty thousand men, that army did what it was put there to do: it kept the peace. And under that peace, at least until the middle of the third Christian century, Dacia prospered, and enjoyed the blessings of Romanization. Cities rose and flourished; an efficient road network was established and maintained; the rich earth was made to yield its store of metals and crops; skilled craftsmen plied their trades; handsome buildings of stone and brick replaced wattle and daub. Amenities—amphitheaters, aqueducts, sewers—were provided; a school of provincial art grew up; literacy —in Latin—was extended. In short, Rome raised this latest of her provinces, as she had the others, from an underdeveloped country to an advanced level of material civilization. That, according to the old-fashioned view, is what empires are for.

But there is a dark side to the picture, which modern Romanian archaeologists and historians emphasize, under the influence not only of Marxist theory, but of the memory of centuries of Hapsburg rule. They point out that under Roman rule there was suffering, oppression, exploitation; they stress the evils of slavery and point out that Rome helped the landowning aristocracy and harmed the poor. They regard the Roman governors, tax collectors, and soldiery as so many machines for grinding down the humble and meek. According to them, the cities exploited the countryside, brigands infested the roads; in no reign was the province free of revolt and invasion.

Though this perhaps overpessimistic view is presented as a novelty, Romanian scholars know perfectly well that the Roman Empire in its own time was not without its critics. The gloomy and rhetorical Roman historian Cornelius Tacitus puts into the mouth of a Scottish chief the standard complaints against the empire: the greedy Romans enslave their subjects; they plunder, they murder, they rape. Coercion is the order of the day: army service, taxation, tribute in kind, the *corvée.* The field, the mines, the ports are Roman; the field hands, the miners, the stevedores are natives. The very concept of empire is a fraud: "They make a desert, and they call it peace."

But Cornelius Tacitus himself served the empire as senator, consul, and proconsul, and the speech he invents for one of his own kind, the legate Cerialis, is a reasonable defense of empire. The aim is peace: you cannot have peace without armies, nor armies without pay, nor pay without taxes. Regimes are not always bad (Trajan was Optimus Princeps, Hadrian a peacemaker; Antoninus was surnamed "the Pious"; Marcus Aurelius was a philosopher; under Septimius Severus Dacia prospered as never before). To err is human: bad emperors are rare and must be treated as acts of God, like a bad harvest or a wet season. The Roman Empire is a linkage, forged by eight hundred years of good luck and hard discipline; if you try to break the links, you will yourselves be broken. Revolt means ruin; obedience means security. Those were hard words and no comfort to rebels, but most Dacians were not rebels: they behaved and Rome let them rule themselves in the new cities with minimum interference from governors or soldiery. On balance, the bourgeoisie at least were materially better off than they had been under Decebalus, nor was resentment of Roman rule strong enough to inspire another national resistance hero. When Rome withdrew in A.D. 271, the Dacians were free, and they tried to carry on in the ways the Romans had taught them, but they did not prosper; when they finally succumbed to the very barbarian invasions that the Roman legions had staved off for so long, those Dacians who knew their history must have felt a certain nostalgia for the Roman peace.

Romanization is essentially a culture of cities. Roman Dacia had eleven, all developed from Trajanic camps. The first and most im-

portant was Ulpia Traiana, the original capital, which began in 101–
2[1] as a camp at a strategic road center five miles east of the Iron
Gates of Transylvania. Between 108 and 110 there grew up on the
site of the camp a colony of Roman citizens, mostly veterans, who received the signal honor of being enrolled in Trajan's own "tribe"
(voting district), the Papiria. The colony was walled like a camp, in
a rectangle with rounded, towered corners (fig. 5.2), enclosing
eighty acres; that is, large enough to hold a population of fifteen
to twenty thousand. The walls, built of squared blocks laid as
headers and stretchers, were thirteen to sixteen feet high, six feet
thick, and protected by a ditch sixteen to twenty feet deep.

Within the walls, near the center of the colony, three important
areas have been excavated. The first is the Aedes Augustalium—the
palace of the priests of the imperial cult—almost unique in the empire (one has recently been excavated at Herculaneum, near Pompeii,
and another at Misenum). Freedmen—ex-slaves—served the cult;
they felt compensated, by the honor of the priesthood, for being cut
off from office-holding as magistrates or town councilors. The building, planned like the headquarters of a Roman camp, is a vast
rectangular tile-roofed complex, with buttressed walls, two stories
high, measuring 279 by 213 feet. One first entered a square court
flanked by dining halls, with an altar to the emperor in the middle.
Behind the square court ran another, long and narrow, embellished
with statues, with a strongroom at one end and a storeroom at the
other. Behind it in turn was centered the shrine of Rome and
Augustus, with vaulted cisterns beneath. On either side of the shrine
were living quarters for the priests, a centrally heated meeting room,
and, slightly off-center, a passage leading to the forum basilica. The
interior walls were roughcast and painted, with Pompeian red the
predominant color.

The forum is the second important intramural area, only partly
excavated. Its basilica, 279 by 32 feet, is long and narrow. It had
marble-revetted walls and was adorned with statues, including one of
a governor at the east end. The forum itself was 138 feet wide and
paved with slate; its total length has not been excavated. Beside the
governor's statue a flight of stairs led to a heated chamber that may

---

1. Henceforward all dates are A.D. unless otherwise noted.

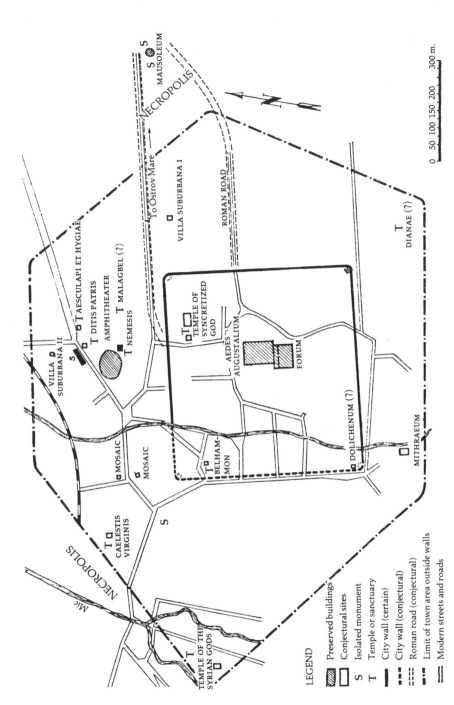

NECROPOLIS

Mic

TEMPLE OF THE
SYRIAN GODS

CAELESTIS
VIRGINIS T

S

MOSAIC

MOSAIC

VILLA
SUBURBANA II

S

AMPHITHEATER

T AESCULAPI ET HYGIAE
T DITIS PATRIS
T MALAGBEL (?)
T NEMESIS

BELHAM-
MON T

DOLICHENUM (?)

TEMPLE OF
SYNCRETIZED
GOD

AEDES
AUGUSTALIUM

FORUM

MITHRAEUM

DIANAE (?)
T

To Ostrov Mare

VILLA SUBURBANA I

ROMAN ROAD

NECROPOLIS

S S
S MAUSOLEUM

N

0 50 100 150 200 300 m.

LEGEND

Preserved buildings
Conjectural sites
S   Isolated monument
T   Temple or sanctuary
         City wall (certain)
         City wall (conjectural)
         Roman road (conjectural)
         Limit of town area outside walls
         Modern streets and roads

5.2. Ulpia Traiana, plan

have been the meeting place of the town council, and, beginning with the reign of Alexander Severus (222–35), of that of the whole, by then tripartite, province.

The third important intramural complex is the baths (not shown on the plan); they were in the northeast corner, dated by tile stamps to 158. The building measures 92 by 75 feet, and has two sets of installations (cold plunge, warm baths, hot baths), one for men and one for women. Roman baths were the poor man's club: some of the rooms may have been used for massage, reading, and games.

The colony expanded outside its original walls. Eight of its eleven temples are extramural; two suburban villas have been excavated, as well as a mausoleum nearly seventy feet in diameter, the last resting place of a young girl of a family prominent in civic affairs in the mid-second century, the Aurelii, who bore the same name as the philosopher-emperor.

But the most impressive building outside the walls is the amphitheater (fig. 5.3), one of three now excavated in Dacia (the others

5.3. Ulpia Traiana, amphitheater

are at Porolissum and Micia). It was stone-built, to hold five thousand. It dates from the earliest years of the colony; stamped tiles show that it was repaired under Antoninus Pius, in 158. Some of the seats bear inscribed initials, reserving them for the Augustales and other local dignitaries. The excavators found a hoard of coins of the fourth century; they also found that the amphitheater's entrances had been blocked in antiquity, making it into a fortress against barbarian invasion at about the time the hoard was hidden. To such straits was Ulpia Traiana reduced after the Roman withdrawal.

But for over one hundred years (Hadrian to Philip the Arab: 117–249) the colony prospered. Part of the evidence is to be seen in the statues and reliefs that crowd the small site museum and the Hunedoara provincial museum at Deva, thirty-five miles to the north. Other evidence comes from inscriptions that reveal a flourishing economic life. The craftsmen mentioned included masons, potters, tilers, silversmiths, furriers, tailors, stonecutters, bakers, and barbers. Evidence for agricultural prosperity comes from the two suburban villas already mentioned, and from a *villa rustica*—a working farm with its buildings, where crops were raised for the market—at Hobiţa, just southeast of the colony. Figure 5.4 gives plans of these three, plus eleven others, all drawn to the same scale.[2] The larger suburban villa at Ulpia Traiana (villa suburbana II, fig. 5.2), 150 meters north of the amphitheater, was sited to command a handsome mountain view. It had seven rooms with tiled floors and painted walls. Both it and its five-room neighbor to the southeast went up in

---

2. The known Dacian villae rusticae cluster mainly around Ulpia Traiana and Napoca (now Cluj). Near the former are the three already mentioned, plus the five-room house at Cincis, and the fourteen-room one of Caracalla's time (211-17) at Mănerau. Near Napoca are the villas at Gîrbau (seven rooms), Dezmir (six rooms), Apahida (two rooms, in use during Septimius Severus's reign, 193-211), Turcea (thirteen rooms), and Aiton (four rooms). The two villas (two and four rooms) at Răhău lie south of Apulum (Alba Iulia), where few would be expected, since its territory was the property of the military, while the villas were privately owned. The modest two-room villa at Moreşti, near Cristeşti, lies apart from the rest, in the Mureş valley, an area where the archaeological evidence is more Dacian than Roman. There must be many others awaiting discovery: the neighboring province of Pannonia (modern Hungary) has 153. The Romanian villas are more humble than those known from other provinces: no mosaics, nor (usually) frescoes, though the ten-room villa at Aiud (ancient Brucla) has central heating and running water.

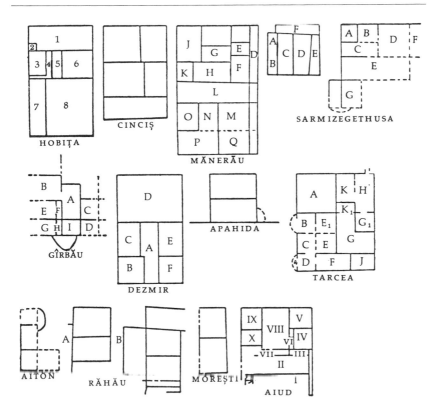

5.4. Villae rusticae, plans

flames during Marcus Aurelius's wars with a German tribe, the
Marcomanni (162–72, 177–80), but were afterward rebuilt on a
more modest scale.

The villa rustica at Hobița was more extensive. The main house
shown in figure 5.4 stands in the northeast corner of a walled area
of fourteen acres. From a tower bonded to the inner face of the wall
on the east, overseers could keep an eye on the slaves working in the
estate fields beyond, and also be on the watch for incursions of
brigands. Coins and pottery date the active life of the estate from the
early years of Antoninus Pius (138–61) to Elagabalus (217–22).
The evidence of the wall and tower for a sense of insecurity during
these years, so close to a provincial center, is highly significant. The

main house, with its seven rooms and courtyard (8 on fig. 5.4) is comfortable without being ostentatious: its occupant was probably the bailiff for a landlord who lived in the town. It had a tile roof, stuccoed interior walls, and two large workrooms. Its unusual amenities include a bath, marble doorframes, frescoes, and imported tableware. Adjoining it, in the center of the walled area, is a corral with two slave barracks; built against the inner face of the wall on the north and northeast were sheds for animals, tools, and farm machinery: a plowshare was among the finds. The location of the villa matches the specifications of the Roman agricultural writer Columella (writing between A.D. 60 and 65). It is near a large town, so that slaves could be used for urban occupations in the winter; and it is near but not on a main road, so that it has the advantage of easy communications with a reduced risk of attacks by highwaymen.

Ulpia Traiana was the financial, religious, and legislative center of the province, which as early as 124 was divided into three: Porolissensis, administered from Napoca; Superior—later renamed Apulensis—administered from Apulum, where the military governor of all three subdivisions had his headquarters; and Inferior—later Malvensis—the site of whose administrative center is uncertain; perhaps it was at Romula. Ulpia Traiana was the seat of the imperial procurator (finance officer) for all three subdivisions. The Aedes Augustalium symbolizes its importance as a religious center for the imperial cult. Its many other temples, and its inscriptions, mostly dedications to Oriental gods (to be discussed in chapter 8), show what a melting pot it was. Businessmen flocked here from all over the empire. From at least the reign of Alexander Severus (222–35) it was, as we saw, the seat of the Council of the Three Dacias, presided over by the chief priest of the Augustales.

The very founding of Ulpia Traiana signified that the Romans were in Dacia to stay. Hadrian, who visited it at the beginning of his reign, in 117–18, added an element to its name that propagandized a wished-for continuity between Dacian and Roman rule: henceforward it was styled Colonia Ulpia Traiana Augusta Dacica Sarmizegethusa, taking over, the Romans hoped, the former prestige of Decebalus's ruined capital, forty-five miles away across the mountains to the east. Hadrian later (132–33) paid for an aqueduct for the colony. Under Alexander Severus, Ulpia Traiana was permitted to style itself, grandiloquently, "metropolis." After the middle of the third century it began to decline: crafts decayed, production fell, inflation ran rampant, poverty was endemic, but there was no money for welfare. The latest coins bear the effigy of Gallienus (260–68). When the Romans withdrew in 271, the natives stayed, eking out a miserable existence, as the pathetic attempt to fortify the amphitheater shows. After the death of Attila the Hun in 453, life in the colony flickered out: fire, rain, frost, earthquake, and stone-robbing took their toll of the buildings; only since 1924 has scientific excavation made it possible to read Ulpia Traiana's story in her stones.

The most important Roman town of south Dacia was Drobeta, now Turnu Severin. Like Ulpia Traiana, it grew up around the site of a Trajanic stone camp, built to hold five hundred men whose job was to guard the head of Apollodorus of Damascus's famous bridge (fig. 5.5). Even earlier, in the first Dacian campaign, Trajan's engineers had built, west of the future site of the bridge, a 37-acre earthwork camp, large enough to hold a whole legion: it lies under the modern railway station. Turnu Severin, a flourishing modern town of over forty thousand, overlies most of the ancient settlement, but the Trajanic stone camp has been excavated and the finds from it and from the bridge are housed in the adjoining Iron Gates Museum. The camp is of the usual playing-card shape, with four towered gates, ten other towers, a headquarters building, storehouses, officers' quarters, and soldiers' barracks. Travelers from the bridge entered by the *porta principalis dextra,* on the west; the area between the camp and the river was walled off to serve as a port. About two hundred meters west of the camp were its baths, supplied by an aqueduct, and open apparently also to civilians. Tile stamps found in them bear the name of the Fifth Macedonian Legion, which was not transferred from Troesmis in Dobruja back to Dacia until 167–68. Besides the baths proper, with the usual succession of warm baths, steam room, and cold plunge, the excavators found an exercise-ground, surrounded by luxurious heated rooms. At Băile Herculane, thirty-five miles to the northwest, hot springs provided a popular resort for rich Romans, which survived into the Hapsburg regime (the state bedchamber of the Emperor Franz Josef and the Empress Elizabeth is

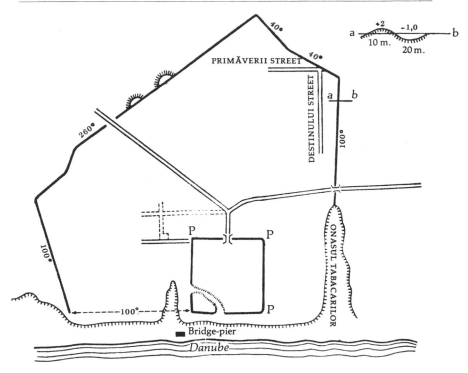

5.5. Drobeta, plan

still shown to visitors) and is a popular spa today. When the rest of Dacia was abandoned in 271, Aurelian retained the bridgehead camp; its later phases will be described in chapter 7.

The civilian town that grew up around the camp was made a *municipium,* with the rights of an Italian town, by Hadrian, perhaps on the occasion of a visit in 123–24, and enrolled in his tribe, the Sergia. It covered sixty-two acres, which means the population was about fourteen thousand. Between 193 and 198, Septimius Severus raised the municipium to the rank of colony, described in an inscription, with the usual overblown language of the age, as *splendidissima.* It was a customs post, but the bureaucrats who ran it were not so predominantly Oriental as those we met at Ulpia Traiana. The cemetery lies inaccessible under the Navy Yard of modern Turnu Severin. Such evidence as there is for the religious beliefs of Drobeta will be described in chapter 8.

Sucidava (now Celei), the third of our Roman towns in Dacia, lies on the Danube 177 miles downstream from Drobeta. There had been a settlement here since Neolithic times. In the Dacian wars, Trajan built an earthwork camp here, probably in connection with the Dobruja campaign: it covered fifteen acres, and would hold half a legion. After the war, a town grew up on the site of the camp. The reign of Philip the Arab was a troubled time for the town, as a hoard of four thousand silver denarii shows. Probably after a raid (245–47) by the Carpi, free Dacians from Moldavia, during Philip's reign, the townsfolk hastily threw up a trapezoidal stone wall (fig. 5.6) and ditch, enclosing sixty-two acres, large enough for a population of nearly fourteen thousand. The wall had rectangular or horseshoe-shaped towers every three hundred feet; towers also flanked the north and south gates. The modern town of Celei overlies ancient Sucidava, so that no street plan or buildings have emerged, but a stretch of Roman road, paved, and with wheel ruts, came to light outside the south gate, near a bronze-worker's shop, identified by the presence in it of copper slag. A kiln proves that pottery was manufactured locally, and inscriptions mention a tanner, a stonecutter, and the owner of a vineyard. Sucidava was a customs station from 180–83 onward: there was a ferry to the south bank, and, later, a Constantinian bridge and a fascinating citadel, which we shall be discussing in chapter 7. Sucidava was a center for the manufacture of lead-backed mirrors. Half of the two hundred such mirrors known in the Roman world come from here, eighty-eight of them from a temple to Bacchus and the nymphs. The discovery of a lead ingot proves they were made here and were not imported. The finds from Sucidava are scattered: some are in the excellent small site-museum in the village schoolhouse, others are in the local museums of Corabia, Caracal, and Orlea, still others are in Craiova and Bucharest.

Sucidava never became a municipium or a colony: its status was always that of a *pagus* or a *vicus,* a simple country town, the market center for a rich *territorium* where thirty settlements are known, stretching northward on the west side of the Olt (in Latin, Alutus) valley till they met the territorium of Romula. When Aurelian abandoned Dacia in 271, he kept a foothold in Sucidava: its history is unbroken down into the seventh century.

Romula, the largest Roman town in south Dacia, and the only one

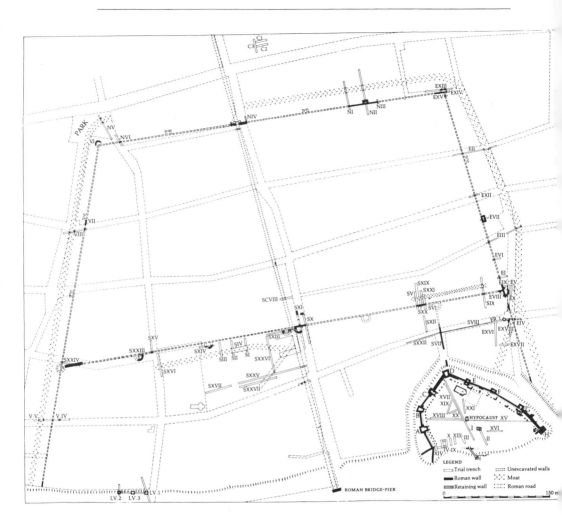

5.6. Sucidava, town, and Constantinian citadel, plan

except Ulpia Traiana to bear a Roman name, lies some thirty-six
miles north of Sucidava, on the Roman road up the Olt valley. L. F.
Marsigli,[3] an Italian engineer in Austrian service who visited the
site in 1691, saw and drew plans of two camps (northeast quadrant,
fig. 5.7), but all trace of these has now disappeared. They were
probably Trajanic. Nowadays the village of Reşca-Dobrosloveni overlies the civil settlement, but careful excavation since 1965 has revealed much of its ancient plan.

In its first phase it was an earthwork (EFGQT), dating probably
from directly after Trajan's Dacian wars. Within this area were excavated an underground aqueduct (EF), and luxurious, marble-
veneered baths (Q). In the reign of Septimius Severus (193–211),
the earthwork was replaced by a brick wall. In its third phase, dated
by an inscription to 248, in the reign of Philip the Arab, the walled
area was greatly extended: its gates have been identified (HILL[1]).
The walls enclosed a pentagonal area of 158 acres, large enough for
a population of forty thousand. The walls, though they were equipped
with towers at intervals of about two hundred feet, bear evidence
of hasty construction, more a flimsy gesture against the threat of
barbarian invasion than a genuine fortification. Within the wall, the
cardo of the city has been traced from the cross-wall gate (K) to
the north (H). The cross-wall, KU, divides the city into two, perhaps one area for the Dacians, and one for the Roman colonists.

The building just south of the cross-wall, at S, was perhaps the
curia, or town hall, with a portico of Corinthian columns, hypocaust
heating, and a tile roof and floor. The excavator dates it in the early
third century.

The city had two cemeteries. In the one to the north (necropolis,
beyond the north gate [H], on the plan), the 150 cremation-

3. This remarkable man (1658–1730) served Eugene of Savoy, the joint
victor with Marlborough of the battles of Blenheim and Malplaquet. While on
the Danube to build a pontoon bridge at Turnu Severin (on the site of Trajan's), he used the occasion to travel widely in Oltenia, and drew plans of
many Roman sites now destroyed. After a quarrel with Eugene he retired to
Bologna and devoted himself to writing a remarkable history of the lower
Danube valley: *Danubius Pannonico-Mysicus: Observationibus Geographicis,
Astronomicis, Hydrographicis, Historicis, Physicis Perlustratus,* 6 vols. (Amsterdam and The Hague, 1726). A French translation appeared in 1744. The Romanian material is in volume 2.

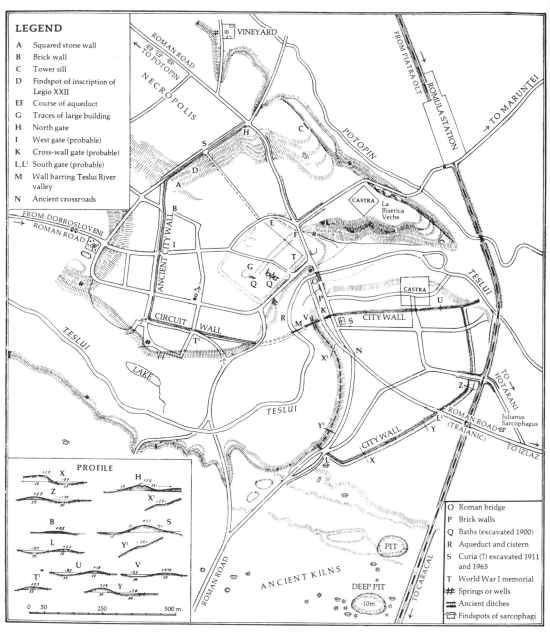

LEGEND

A   Squared stone wall
B   Brick wall
C   Tower sill
D   Findspot of inscription of
    Legio XXII
EF Course of aqueduct
G   Traces of large building
H   North gate
I   West gate (probable)
K   Cross-wall gate (probable)
L,L¹ South gate (probable)
M   Wall barring Teslui River
    valley
N   Ancient crossroads

O   Roman bridge
P   Brick walls
Q   Baths (excavated 1900)
R   Aqueduct and cistern
S   Curia (?) excavated 1911
    and 1965
T   World War I memorial
Springs or wells
    Ancient ditches
    Findspots of sarcophagi

PROFILE

0   50   250   500 m.

5.7. Romula, plan

graves excavated yielded few grave goods: the assumption is that this was the burial place of the Dacian poor. The cemetery to the south was much richer, with roadside plots equipped with stone benches, and sarcophagi in wood, lead, or stone. Of these, the one that contained the mortal remains of a certain Aelius Julius Julianus was found southeast of Z on the plan, and is now on display in the courtyard of the Caracal museum. An account is preserved of its discovery and opening in 1836. A farmer digging a trench found it in a vaulted chamber, its lid held down by four iron spikes sealed with lead. Opened, the sarcophagus proved to contain the embalmed body of a man lying on a bed of laurel leaves. He had good teeth, and curly chestnut hair, on which he wore a gold coronet representing laurel and oak leaves. A bronze medallion hung around his neck, and his leather shoes were decorated with glass studs. The inscription on the sarcophagus states that he had served as decurion, quaestor, and aedile (town councilor, treasurer, and mayor) of the colony. (Romula became a municipium perhaps in Hadrian's reign, and a colony under Septimius Severus [193–211].) Below are inscribed some trite but touching verses commissioned by his widow: he lived blamelessly for forty years; now she and their children have laid him in this shaded green plot among the vineyards. "Traveler, pray that the earth lie light upon him."

The prosperity that paid for the sarcophagus came from agriculture, especially viticulture, as the epitaph implies. (Vineyards still flourish in the Olt valley: my host in a village near Romula was up at five in the morning at vintage time "to scare the birds from my grapes.") The *territorium* of Romula was—and is—fertile: twenty-five Daco-Roman communities, which have yielded numerous finds of farm tools, are known in the area, between the Olt and the Jiu. Prosperity paid for luxury imports, on which duties were paid to the local Roman customs officer: *terra sigillata* from Italy, Gaul, and Germany; olive oil and wine from Greece, in amphoras stamped with Greek names on the handles; bronze lamps and statuettes; glassware, jewelry (one of the finds was the remains of a little wooden jewel box with gold handles).

Craftsmen flourished in Romula, too. Kilns, molds, and the finished product—vases, lamps, tiles, water pipe, figurines, masks, and mortars with bits of flint set in the bottom for grinding grain—

show that pottery was made locally. Loom weights and spindles establish weaving and spinning as household industries; clay sinkers are evidence for fishing in the local river, the Teslui, and the Olt, whose course ran closer to Romula in antiquity than today. But Romula's unique craft was intaglio, the carving of designs on semiprecious stones: Fortuna (Lady Luck), the emperor, and empress, a shepherd with a lamb, on jasper, onyx, sardonyx, cornelian, rock crystal. One stone, bearing the likeness of Melpomene, the Greek tragic muse, suggests not only a high cultural level, but the possibility that Romula had a theater, as yet undiscovered. Some of the gems are inscribed: "Bon Voyage" and "Forget-Me-Not" (in Greek) and "Beware of the Dog" (in Latin).

Greek inscriptions are rare in Dacia—only thirty-seven out of a total of three thousand—but Romula has produced a graffito that is rarer still: a dedication, on the base of a clay statuette, in the Semitic alphabet, to the Syrian goddess Atargatis. The subject of religion in ancient Romania is reserved for the final chapter, but here it is appropriate to remark that dedications to Oriental gods show what a melting pot Romula was: the divinities honored, apart from the Greco-Roman pantheon, include the Thracian Rider; the Danubian Rider; Cybele the Earth Mother, from Asia Minor; Mithras, the Persian god of light (no fewer than thirty examples: he was a great favorite with soldiers); Isis and Sarapis from Egypt, and Atargatis and Turmasgadis (a cult title of Ba'al, syncretized with Jupiter) from Palmyra in Syria.

Yet the dedication to Roman gods shows that Romanization was proceeding apace: only Juno, Vesta, Neptune, and Vulcan are missing from the pantheon; among lesser divinities we find Aesculapius with Hygieia; Flora, Fortuna, Hercules, Nemesis, the Nymphs, Pan, Pomona, Priapus, the Satyrs, Silenus, Silvanus, and Victoria. The inscriptions prove literacy in Latin, an important part of Romanization.

But Romulans were not to be left to worship in peace. The building of the third phase of the town wall, in 248, was a defensive measure against the invading Carpi, and the finding of a huge hoard of eight thousand coins, ranging in date from Commodus to Elagabalus (180–222) shows that insecurity antedated the mid-third century. Romula was abandoned in 271, and did not revive until Constantine. Its most tangible evidence of survival, the finds from the

site, are best to be seen in the museums of Caracal and Bucharest
(the gems), Corabia, Craiova, and Turnu Severin.

From Romula, the possible capital of Dacia Inferior/Malvensis, we
move to Apulum (now Alba Iulia), the capital of Dacia Superior/
Apulensis, and the military headquarters of the whole tripartite
province. Most of what we know of ancient Apulum must be derived
from the finds in the rich local museum on the citadel height, since
the modern town of over twenty thousand is built over the ancient
remains, and is itself a historical monument: here in 1599 Michael
the Brave proclaimed the unification of Romania; here in 1918 the
union of Transylvania, formerly Austro-Hungarian, with Romania
was ratified; here in 1922 King Ferdinand and Queen Marie were
crowned. The place was historically important from its Roman beginnings. The citadel, built in the eighteenth century by Visconti
under the supervision of Eugene of Savoy, overlies the vast Roman
camp of sixty to seventy-five acres (fig. 5.8) that was the headquarters of the Legio XIII Gemina, Dacia's permanent army of occupation. The governor operated from here, beginning in 118–19; so
did the procurator (finance officer) of Dacia Superior/Apulensis,
from 124, and it was military headquarters for all Dacia from 168.
Perhaps to an army surgeon belonged the 34-piece medical kit found
at Apulum: it included probes, needles, a scalpel, a spoon, a spatula,
and tweezers.

As the plan makes clear, there were at Apulum, in addition to the
military headquarters, two civil settlements. The municipium, on the
low ground north and east of the camp, must have grown up in
Trajan's reign, for it was assigned to his tribe, the Papiria, but the
first surviving mention of it is dated in Commodus's reign, after 180.
The colony, which was also the port, lay south of the camp, in the
Partoş quarter, on the Mureş River. The building of the railway, in
1886–87, wrought much havoc among its ancient buildings. It
flourished in the second and third centuries. One building in it,
measuring 164 by 48 feet, is a curiosity: it contained the workrooms
of a number of different craftsmen. The 361 bone needles found
there were used by a furrier; the weaver had a trough to wash his
cloth; the potter had his kiln. There were also baths attached, and
living quarters above. Inscriptions, of uncertain provenience, record

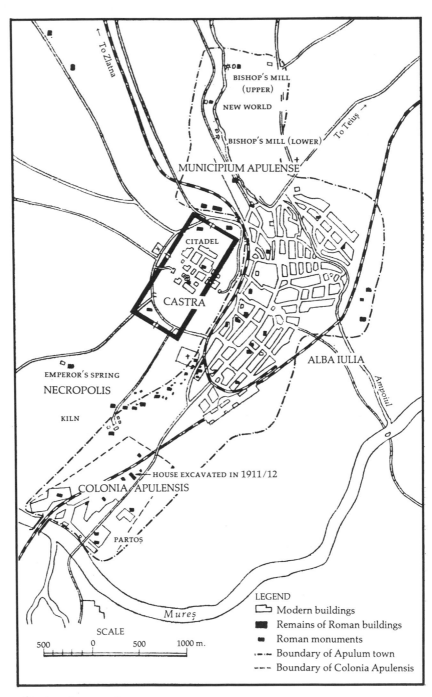

To Zlatna

BISHOP'S MILL (UPPER)

NEW WORLD

To Teiuș →

BISHOP'S MILL (LOWER)

MUNICIPIUM APULENSE

CITADEL

CASTRA

EMPEROR'S SPRING

NECROPOLIS

ALBA IULIA

Ampoiul

KILN

HOUSE EXCAVATED IN 1911/12

COLONIA APULENSIS

PARTOȘ

Mureș

LEGEND

⬜ Modern buildings

◼ Remains of Roman buildings

■ Roman monuments

▪▬▪ Boundary of Apulum town

▬ ▬ ▬ Boundary of Colonia Apulensis

SCALE

500   0   500   1000 m.

5.8. Apulum, plan

a basilica, an aqueduct, fountains, public baths, and temples, to gods Greco-Roman, Persian, Celtic (Bussumarus), Punic (Tanit), and Anatolian (Dolichenus and Sabazius). A crude graffito of a gladiator, carrying a trident, and labeled Herculanus, has been used, unconvincingly, to argue that Apulum had an amphitheater.

Apulum had at least three cemeteries, one southwest of the camp, one along the road that led northwest to the gold mines of Ampelum (modern Zlatna), and one on the citadel height, under the Orthodox cathedral. The last of these is the best-reported. It contained thirty inhumations, dated by coins from Trajan to Faustina the Younger, the wife of Marcus Aurelius: she died in 175. The burials in the middle of the cemetery were in brick sarcophagi, for the rich; those around the edges were of wood, for the poor. The grave furniture included lamps, keys, hairpins, pots, and a headless stone eagle. There were also twelve cremation-graves, without ash-urns, and therefore of the poor. They contained a few pots, a silver ring, and coins from Trajan to Antoninus Pius, who died in 161. The clearest evidence of Romanization at Apulum is a second-century gravestone with a relief (fig. 5.9) of the she-wolf suckling Romulus and Remus, the twin founders of Rome.

5.9. Apulum, wolf and twins, relief

About fifty miles north of Apulum, on the military road to the northern frontier, lay Potaissa, now Turda, an industrial town of 65,000. A dated milestone from Aiton, seven miles farther north, shows that the road was in use at least as early as 107–8. The camp, just southwest of the modern town, covered fifty-three acres, large enough for two legions. Coins show that it was in use from the time of Trajan to at least that of Marcia Otacilia Severa, the wife of Philip the Arab (244–49). A native settlement (*canabae*) grew up at the camp gates; it increased in importance when in 167–68 Marcus Aurelius, fighting his war against the Marcomanni to the north, transferred Legio V Macedonica here from Troesmis in Dobruja, and made Potaissa the military headquarters of Dacia Porolissensis. Under Septimius Severus Potaissa became a municipium, under Caracalla a colony. Its prosperity was based on salt and gold: one can still go from here—by narrow-gauge train—to the old gold-mining town of Alburnus Maior (now Roşia Montană, near Abrud), fifty miles to the southwest. A set of twenty-five wax tablets discovered in the mine shafts there has much to tell us about the lives of the miners between 131 and 167. The tablets are described in the last chapter.

One way or another, but mostly from inscriptions, we know that the town had an aqueduct, baths—enlarged in 195, during the Severan prosperity—and a basilica, dating in a first or second phase as late as the reign of Gordian III (238–44). Religious dedications reveal what must by now seem the usual mixture of races: among those who lived and worked in Potaissa were Egyptians, Pannonians, Italians, Illyrians, Thracians, and Phrygians. Coins and pottery show that the town lived on, still with a Roman air about it, after Aurelian's withdrawal from Dacia in 271. A large necropolis in Potaissa's territorium, a dozen miles to the northeast, shows by pottery dated after 271 that the natives stayed when the Romans left.

Thirty miles up the military road north from Potaissa lay Napoca, now Cluj, the capital of Transylvania, with a population of over 205,000. It is a city full of old-world charm, with many reminders— the palace, the splendid fourteenth-century Gothic church of St. Michael—that it was Austro-Hungarian until 1918. Like its Daco-Roman predecessor, it is a melting pot: one hears much German

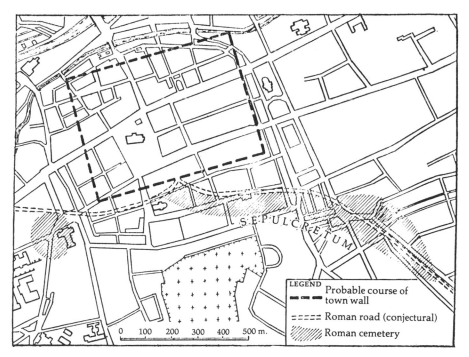

LEGEND
▬ ▬ ▬ Probable course of town wall
===== Roman road (conjectural)
▨▨▨ Roman cemetery

0 100 200 300 400 500 m.

5.10. Napoca, plan

spoken; the elder generation refers to it by its German name, Klausenburg, or its Hungarian one, Kolosvar; there are a Hungarian newspaper, theater, and opera house. And its fine Museum of History, crammed with Dacian and Roman finds,[4] is a center of vigorous archaeological investigation, with Hadrian Daicoviciu directing an energetic and productive team of excavators.

Unfortunately the Roman remains *in situ* are slight, limited to occasional finds of walls during building operations, and to what inscriptions have to tell. Hadrian visited Napoca in 124, and made it a municipium, attached to his tribe, the Sergia; Commodus made it a colony. The extent of its walls is known, enclosing eighty acres (fig. 5.10), and Roman remains were found under St. Michael's, in the spacious Piața Libertații, which was probably the ancient forum. The

4. Not so crammed as it used to be. The chief treasures of all the provincial museums in Romania were requisitioned in 1971–72 to enrich the new Museum of National History in Bucharest.

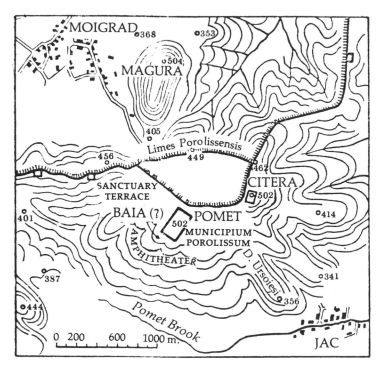

5.11. Porolissum, plan

rectangle of the town walls has the shape of the original Roman
camp. Napoca was the seat of the procurator of Dacian Porolissensis. Its artisans, merchants, and magistrates included, to judge
from the dedications to their gods, Galatians, Carians, Syrians, Thracians, Illyrians, and Celts. One town official rivaled Pooh-Bah in
pluralism: he held magistracies in Napoca, Apulum, Drobeta,
Dierna, and Porolissum. Napoca's territorium was large and fertile:
we know of thirteen villae rusticae within it. The proprietor of the
one at Ciumăfaia, ten miles north-northeast of Napoca, was a retired
centurion who had also been mayor of the town. Coins of Aurelian—
extremely rare in Dacia—show that economic life went on in Napoca
down to the abandonment of the province; coins of the Emperor
Tacitus (275–76), and of Crispus (son of Constantine the Great,
appointed Caesar in 317) show that it continued thereafter.

The Dacian terminus of the great military road through the heart of the province to Aquincum (Budapest) in Pannonia was Porolissum (now Moigrad), near Zalău, in the județ of Sălaj. Like other Dacian towns, this one grew up around a camp, but Porolissum is unique in having two camps, adjacent to a regular walled frontier, like the German *limes* (fig. 5.11),[5] the only such stretch so far discovered in Dacia. The larger camp, on the height called Pomet, measures 965 by 873 feet, large enough for four thousand men. Its original earthwork phase is Trajanic; it was rebuilt in stone in the reign of Antoninus Pius (138–61), with walls five feet thick. The camp was refurbished on the occasion of a visit by Caracalla in 213, at which time the townsfolk put up a bronze equestrian statue of him, fragments of which are on display in the Museum of National History in Bucharest; figure 5.12 shows what is left of the head of this cruel and fratricidal monarch. There were further repairs in 251. The

5. See MacKendrick, *Romans on the Rhine*, fig. 4.1.

5.12. Porolissum, Caracalla, bronze head

smaller camp, on the height called Citera, measures only 330 by 220 feet; it would hold a detachment of five hundred. Like Pomet, it began as an earthwork, but it was destroyed in the Marcomannic War, and rebuilt in stone, with walls four feet thick. The limes is an earthwork with ditch, facing north, with watch- and signal-towers at regular intervals, like the milecastles on the Antonine turf wall from Forth to Clyde in Scotland. Its course has been traced for several kilometers. Near the Pomet and Citera camps it is doubled; the re-entrant angle stretch shown on the plan is stone-built, without towers. Perhaps it served as a detention area, where travelers crossing the frontier in either direction would have their papers examined and their baggage searched.

The civil settlement of Porolissum grew up south and east of the Pomet camp, though there had been a Dacian village on the Măgura height to the north, cut off from the new canabae by the limes-wall (fig. 5.11). Northwest of Pomet was the Sanctuary Terrace, with a round shrine of Liber Pater, the Dacian equivalent of the Roman wine-god Bacchus. Southwest of Pomet, on the Palaestra Terrace, were bath buildings, for the use of the soldiers and perhaps of the civilian population as well. To the southwest of the baths lay the amphitheater, one of the three now known in Dacia, or four, if the Apulum gladiator-graffito is to be taken as evidence. It is slightly smaller than the one at Ulpia Traiana: its arena is some 23 feet shorter; its length is 196 feet as compared with 219 for the other. It was rebuilt in stone in 157. These camp amphitheaters were primarily intended for military training, but no doubt the civilian population was entertained. there with gladiatorial shows from time to time.

Porolissum was made a municipium in the reign of Septimius Severus; it never achieved colonial status. One multipurpose block, like the one at Apulum, is of interest. It was hypocaust-heated; its twenty-one rooms included a vestibule, an atrium, a bakery, kitchens, shops, storerooms, living quarters, and a latrine. The town cemetery was on the Ursoieș hill, to the south. The finds from it are poverty-stricken, dated in the second century.

Porolissum, despite the protection of the limes, was, as the Roman outpost farthest north, especially exposed to attack. It was the first Roman town in Dacia to suffer. Its last documents come from two

5.13. Ulpia Traiana, Decius, bronze head

reigns. The first is that of Decius (249–51) who took the surname Trajan, and is famous for his last-ditch attempts at the defense of Dacia, and notorious for his persecution of the Christians. The head (fig. 5.13) of his statue in bronze, discovered at Ulpia Traiana and now on display in the Bucharest museum, is of artistic interest because of the evidence all over its surface that it had been patched in antiquity. The very last documents of Porolissum as part of the Roman province are coins from the reign of Gallienus (263–68), but Roman coinage began to circulate again under Valentinian I (364–75) and Valens (emperor in the East, 364–78).

The last three important towns of Roman Dacia must be described more briefly, for lack of excavation or of published reports. They are Dierna (Orşova), Tibiscum (Jupa, near Caransebeş), and Ampelum (Zlatna). Dierna lay west of Drobeta, five miles upstream from the Iron Gates. Today the building of the dam and hydroelectric plant at the Iron Gates has caused a whole new town to rise on the ancient site. It was, as we saw in the last chapter, one of Trajan's base camps in his First Dacian War; it became a customs station; by Severus's reign it was a municipium. Its topography is quite unknown, but coins show that after the end of Roman Dacia it lived on till the reign of Arcadius (383–408).

Tibiscum we saw to have been also important to Trajan in the Dacian wars. Its earthwork camp, covering five and a half acres, would hold comfortably a detachment of one thousand men—we hear of Moors and Palmyrenes. Its walls were later rebuilt in brick, with square towers. The Goths sacked it in Gallienus's reign; a hoard of 1,616 Roman bronze coins of the third and fourth centuries shows how precarious was its existence after Aurelian withdrew.

Ampelum was the mining center, like a California gold-rush town. It was the seat of the imperial procurator for the gold mines, and had become a municipium by 200. Miners' tools found here are displayed in the museums of Deva, Brad, Alba Iulia, Cluj, Sibiu, and Blaj. Experts from Dalmatia were brought in to work the mines; we know of one who had a Bedouin wife. Details on the wretched wages and working conditions of the slaves and poor freemen who dug the gold are reserved for the final chapter. The pitiful contents of their graves reveal their poverty. The last evidence of Roman exploitation of the mines dates from 215.

While all these towns were military in origin, they developed as civilian communities. Such prosperity as they enjoyed was due to a complicated system of military defenses, which will now be briefly described, with the help of the map (fig. 5.1). The complex system reflects a complex problem. Dacia, a salient slicing deep into barbarian territory, could not be defended by a single barrier, like Hadrian's Wall in Britain or the Rhine and Upper Danube *limites* in Germany, Rhaetia, Noricum, and Pannonia. In Dacia, there was not only the threat of the barbarians beyond the frontier. The comparatively small, 50,000-man Roman army of occupation had also to keep a watchful eye on the Dacians within the province, in whom Decebalus's spirit of resistance might be by no means dead. And so the Romans stationed detachments in strongholds all over the three subdivisions of Dacia. These can best be discussed geographically, under ten heads. We shall limit ourselves to a few examples of each, partly for the sake of simplicity, partly because the source material is inadequate.

1. *The Dacian heartland: Decebalus's citadels.* / Here the best example is Orăștioara de Sus (Bucium), just north of the ruined citadel of Costești, where, though the camp is much eroded by the river, the northwest corner tower is left, and enough of the west side so that we know it was 426 feet long. A detachment of Germans garrisoned the camp. One of them came from Cologne, as we know from his grave-stele, built into the camp wall when it was repaired in the reign of Elagabalus (217-22; the evidence is a coin). At Sarmizegethusa Dacica itself, the population was evacuated, and Decebalus's buildings systematically destroyed, their stones reused for military purposes. Some of the stone drums from the sanctuaries are still visible, built into the circuit wall, and the Roman army's baths used Dacian blocks. A detachment of Legio IV Flavia and I Adiutrix was here briefly, but withdrawn, perhaps to nearby Bucium, early in Hadrian's reign.

2. *The north bank of the Danube.* / We have already discussed Dierna, Drobeta, and Sucidava: here let us add Desa, sixty miles west of Sucidava, where an inscription shows there was a detachment of the Legio XIII Gemina on station between 275 and 305; the inscription is evidence that, after the official abandonment of the province, the Romans kept enclaves on the north bank.

3. *The West (now called the Banat).* / We have already had occasion to mention Arcidava (Vărădia), whose forty-acre camp would hold two-thirds of a legion. By 157 it had a stone wall and headquarters building, and was garrisoned by a cohort from near Augusta Vindelicum (Augsburg, in Bavaria). It lasted into the third century. Centum Putei (now Surduc), the next camp north, is unexcavated, but we know it was of the same size as Arcidava, and garrisoned in the early days of the province by Legio IV Flavia. Berzobis was mentioned in the last chapter; it carried on as a civilian settlement after the legions left. On the Dierna-Tibiscum road, the forty-acre camp Ad Mediam, now Mehadia, has also been mentioned as the best-preserved camp in the province. Its gates, towers, and praetorium were restored in the reign of Severus Alexander (222-35), and again under Constantine. A civilian settlement, with public baths, stretched east and north of the camp for a kilometer. Evidence of the frontier insecurity of the place, even in the second century, is pro-

vided by an inscription that records how the sons of a town magistrate murdered by highwaymen took vengeance on the assassins.

It is convenient to treat here an important installation on the border between the Banat and Transylvania. This is Micia, now Veţel, about six miles west of Deva. The camp (fig. 5.14), one of the largest in Dacia, measuring 590 by 1,180 feet, has been cut in two by both road and railway. Its earthwork phase was replaced in stone in 157. Over the years it was garrisoned by a remarkable assortment of auxiliary troops: Spaniards, Germans, Swiss (*Alpini*), Moors, Pannonians, Greeks (*Bosporani*), and Arabs. Their job was to police the frontier, collect tolls from the Mureş river traffic, and guard the approaches to the gold mines, which began at Baiţa, only a dozen miles to the north. In 204 the Moorish contingent restored, about a mile southwest of the camp, a temple with a conventional Roman three-cella plan, where they worshiped a trio of unidentified Moorish gods, syncretized with the Roman Capitoline triad, Jupiter, Juno, and Minerva. North of the camp, on the river, was a modest commercial quarter, with shipsheds and workshops. About a furlong east of these were the baths, shared by soldiers and civilians. They were built in the second century, and twice restored under the Severi. Another eighth of a mile east of these, close to the ancient river bank, a series of five pottery kilns testifies to the presence of Dacian artisans, who stayed on after the Romans left: the site has yielded a gold *solidus* of Justinian, who reigned in Constantinople (Byzantium) from 527 to 565; a fibula has been dated a century later. Interesting evidence for literacy is provided by a family grave-stele one of whose figures is a boy with a stylus—for writing on wax tablets—and a satchel to keep the tablets in.

But the most interesting discovery at Micia is a small amphitheater —the third (or fourth) known in Dacia—unearthed in 1968 not far south of the baths. It is only half the size of the one at Porolissum: it would hold about one thousand spectators, who sat on wooden bleachers set in stone footings. Bones of indigenous wild animals— bear, wolf, lion—show what kind of opposition the gladiators faced in the arena. On the evidence of coins, the amphitheater was in use from Hadrian's reign to that of Alexander Severus.

4. *The northwest frontier.* / At Gilău, on the Roman military road nine miles west of Cluj, a Trajanic earthwork held a detachment

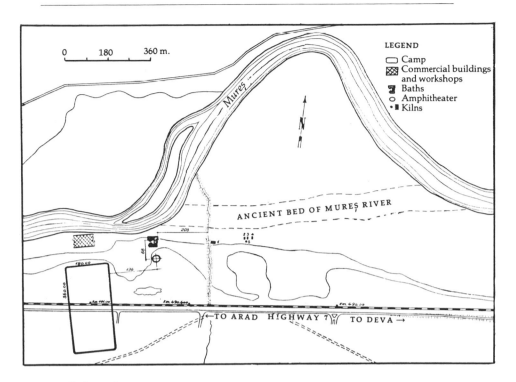

5.14. Micia, plan

of one thousand men. It was rebuilt in stone in 148. Commodus created a no-man's-land five miles deep north of it to discourage the barbarians. He apparently succeeded, for the camp was not abandoned when Aurelian withdrew. The military road continued for another thirty miles northwestward to Resculum (now Bologa), garrisoned by North Africans. Caracalla rebuilt it; a milestone shows that it was still in use in the reign of Maximinus the Thracian (235–38). From Bologa a line of forts and watchtowers, carefully excavated by archaeologists from Cluj, stretched north and east to Porolissum. The best example is Buciumi (not to be confused with Bucium near Costeşti: the name, which means "trumpet" in Romanian, is appropriate for more than one camp site). Of the usual playing-card shape, it covers five and a half acres, and would hold one thousand men. Figure 5.15 shows the remains of one of its towers, facing northwest, toward the barbarian. In Caracalla's reign, when the camp was apparently rebuilt in stone, its garrison came from Britain. There was a headquarters building with a peristyle, warehouses, and six barracks blocks. There were also baths *inside* the camp, which is unusual, but to be explained as a sign not of decadence but of insecurity: with the barbarians so close, baths outside the camp walls would not have been safe.

5. *Southeast from Porolissum.* / Here the map (fig. 5.1) shows a string of nine camps, from Tihău to Odorhei, with one (Gherla) behind the line. Their histories are all roughly similar. Built as earthworks under Trajan, for detachments of five hundred to fifteen hundred men, they were rebuilt in stone under the Antonines, survived into the military anarchy (235–71), and were apparently abandoned thereafter. A few details stand out. It is possible to draw a plan of Căşei, in its 6.6-acre, stone-built phase (fig. 5.16) of about 143. It had horseshoe-shaped towers, a headquarters building, in which weapons were found, and walls with inner spurs, on which the wall-

5.15. Buciumi, tower

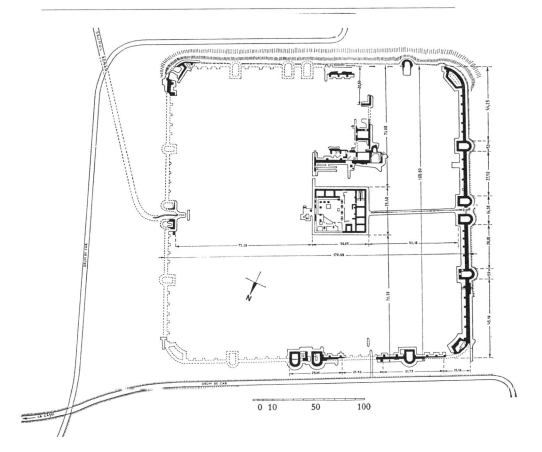

5.16. Căşei, plan

walk rested. Its garrison under Hadrian was Palmyrene; under
Septimius Severus, Britons; under Caracalla, both units did duty as
beneficiarii, a sort of rural gendarmerie. From Gherla, the camp
behind the lines, fifteen miles south of Căşei, comes the important
diploma, or bronze certificate of honorable discharge (fig. 5.17),
dated July 2, 133, whose eighth line surprised scholars by mention-
ing Dacia Porolissensis thirty-five years before they had thought it ex-
isted. The troops from Gherla were moved to Oescus, on the south
bank of the Danube opposite Sucidava, sometime after 260, but before Aurelian's official withdrawal from the province. At Ilişua the

5.17. Gherla, diploma

berm (the stretch between wall and moat) was found paved with
tombstones in reuse. At Orheiul Bistriței there came to light a Dacian
helmet, a sixteen-room bath complex, and the earliest military tile-
kiln known in Dacia, dating from before 150. Elsewhere, native
Dacians operated the kilns. At Inlăceni the gates were blocked as an
emergency measure against barbarian invasion, sometime during the
years of the military anarchy.

6. *East of Transylvania toward the Dobruja border.* / In this area
archaeological excavation has made sense out of the historical record.
This states that Hadrian, the peacemaker, was tempted to give up
Dacia, but was overpersuaded on the ground of the harm this would
do to Roman settlers. What archaeology shows is that Hadrian did in
fact abandon certain Trajanic camps in Muntenia, the area between
the Olt and Dobruja. Mălăeşti, for example, built by Trajan in 101,
was·destroyed, probably by the Romans themselves, early in Hadrian's
reign—the latest coins are of 117—and Drajna de Sus tells the same
story. Hadrian's arrangement with the local tribe, the Roxolani,
whereby they were in effect paid to renounce hostilities, made the
upkeep of these camps henceforth unnecessary. Angustia (now
Breţcu), on the other hand, which guarded the Oituz Pass into the
province of Dacia, was too strategically important to give up. The
twelve-acre camp here, originally an earthwork, was reinforced in
stone and equipped with baths. But its coins cease with Commodus,
so it must, as an outpost, have fallen early. It may have had a garrison as early as Domitian's war against Decebalus: a diploma found
here, granting honorable discharge to members of a naval detachment based in Dobruja, is dated in 92.

7. *The Limes Alutanus.* / Trajan learned in his Dacian wars the
importance of holding the 125-mile line along the west bank of the
Olt, and the lesson did not escape Hadrian, who had been on his
staff. The firmest evidence is inscriptional: it records a detachment at
Buridava (modern Stolniceni) between 105 and 107. Seventy miles
farther south, at Slăveni, Trajan's camp was destroyed by the
Marcomanni, and massively rebuilt by Septimius Severus in 205 (fig.
5.18). A triple ditch defended it; its headquarters building is one of
the most impressive in Dacia, with an apsidal shrine for the legionary
standards, and an armory where spearpoints and arrowheads were
found. The adjoining building was the troops' mess hall and club-
house; the buttressed building next to it was a granary; the other,
flimsier buildings on the plan were barracks. There is evidence
that the camp continued to be occupied after Dacia was officially
abandoned. Twenty miles northeast of Buridava, on the other side of
the Olt, lies Rădăcineşti, a small Hadrianic camp, only 250 feet
square, at which excavation was in progress in the summer of 1971.
Our final example from the Limes Alutanus is Arutela (Bivolari),

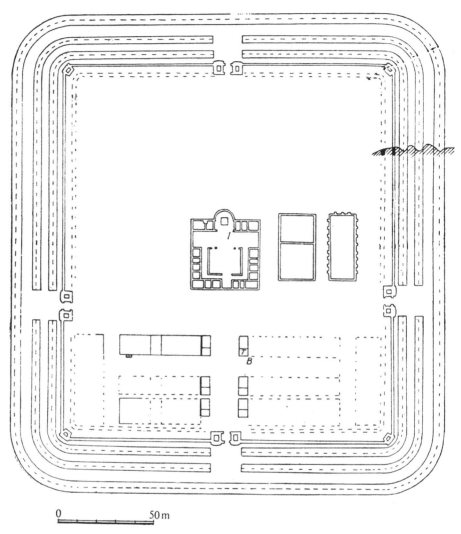

0   50 m

5.18. Slăveni, plan

5.19. View from Arutela

also on the east bank of the Olt, opposite the fourteenth-century Cozia monastery. Nowadays, access to it is by punt, poled by a Charon-like figure in a greenish cloak. Its dimensions are unknown, since the railway and the river have cut away its western half: the measurable eastern side is 210 feet long. The wall has inner spurs that supported the wall-walk. Figure 5.19, a view taken from the camp, shows how it controls the valley here, narrowed by the mountains that descend sharply to the river. It lasted until about 240, when the barbarians destroyed it. Its last coins are of Severus Alexander.

   8. *Oltenia.* / This is the area between the west bank of the Olt and the east bank of the Jiu. Bumbești and Răcari are typical camps: both began as Trajanic earthworks, both are on river banks, both were probably about the same size. The long side of Bumbești measures 548 feet; the long side of Răcari (a 1,000-man camp), 561; more than half of Bumbești has slid into the river. Salvage excava-

tion has revealed part of the headquarters building, containing fragments of a bronze statue of Caracalla, two barracks, two of the towered gates, and exterior baths. Bumbeşti was important because it controlled access through the Vîlcan pass into the Dacian heartland. Septimius Severus rebuilt it in stone in 201. The last coins are of Philip the Arab. Răcari was rebuilt in stone under Hadrian, with corner towers, a monumental praetorium, and a granary. A fragmentary diploma from here, issued in the reign of Antoninus Pius, mentions a detachment of Moors. The excavators found no fewer than three thousand fragments from two bronze statues, one of the hated Elagabalus (217–22). The camp was burned, probably by the Carpi, between 243 and 247, but it was miserably reoccupied by civilians, who enlarged the moat, blocked the gate, and eked out an existence in wooden shacks. Attila and his Huns sacked it between 441 and 443; it finally succumbed to the Avars in the sixth century.

9. *The Limes Transalutanus.* / Septimius Severus pushed Dacia's eastern frontier six to nine miles east of the Olt, constructing a series of fourteen camps, over a distance of 140 miles, beginning at Flăminda on the Danube and stretching northward to Cumidava (now Rîşnov), which had a military road link with Angustia (Breţcu), already mentioned as the farthest east of the Roman camps in Dacia. The evidence of excavation is that the Limes Transalutanus did not last much beyond the reign of Gordian III: it was probably abandoned in the face of the invasion of the Carpi. The best-reported site is Jidava (Cîmpulung), where a Limes Museum is planned. Jidava would have held a 500-man detachment, protected by a double ditch, and a wall six feet thick and originally over thirteen feet high, with corner and curtain towers. Within were the usual headquarters building, with armory and a granary. The camp streets were paved with river-pebbles. The excavators report that it was abandoned in haste and destroyed by fire about the middle of the third century.

10. *The gold-mining country.* / Since the sites at Ampelum (Zlatna) and Alburnus Maior (Roşia Montană) have been mentioned already, let us simply remember that the gold mines had been one of the major attractions of Dacia for the Romans from the beginning. Army detachments were posted there to keep a watchful eye on the miners, whose working conditions were such as to make revolt a constant threat.

The story has been long and complicated, but the conclusion is simple: it bears out Cerealis's logic of imperialism, mentioned near the beginning of the chapter: peacekeeping the end in view, the army the means, taxation to pay the army the middle term. To protect a dozen towns—and their own interests—the Romans kept fifty thousand men, mostly non-Roman auxiliaries, on the alert in a hundred camps for 165 years. The withdrawal under Aurelian in 271 was largely of administrators and landed proprietors: the poorer Dacians stayed on, making what use they could, usually without the protection of the Roman army, of the techniques they had learned from their conquerors. Dacia was free, but the Dacians were Romanized. They are so today, and that is the most lasting result of five generations of Roman rule.

6.1. Callatis–Rome treaty

6. DOBRUJA
125 B.C. – A.D. 275

When we last looked at Histria, Tomis, and Callatis, the Greek coastal cities of Dobruja, the time was the late second century B.C. and they were in their late-Hellenistic doldrums, dependent for their defense upon native chiefs. In the late second and early first centuries B.C. the Pontic cities fell under the sway of Mithridates VI of Pontus: his name appears on their coins; he used their ports as naval bases. Being under the thumb of Mithridates meant running afoul of Rome, for the king's expansionist policies ran counter to Rome's interests in the east. The Roman general M. Terentius Varro Lucullus imposed upon Callatis, in 72–71 B.C., a treaty of alliance, the text of which survives in part (fig. 6.1). It is the oldest extant Latin inscription from eastern Europe, and is on display in the Museum of National History in Bucharest. It appears to be a treaty of mutual assistance and of neutrality; i.e., each party pledges itself to give no aid to any enemy of the other. It provides for revision, if both parties agree, and for public display of the text in Callatis and Rome. The specified location in Rome is the Temple of Concord, which was used for the purpose between 83 and 69 B.C., while the usual posting place, the Capitoline temple, was being rebuilt after a fire. Hence the date given above. It is likely that Rome struck similar treaties with Tomis and Histria, since she needed all three ports as advanced bases for control both of the Black Sea and of the Thraco-Macedonian frontier.

But ten years after the Callatis treaty, the extortions of the proconsul of Macedonia, C. Antonius Hybrida, provoked revolt in the Pontic cities; in coalition with native tribes, the Bastarnae and the Getae, they beat him decisively before the walls of Histria in 61 B.C.

Their freedom, however, was destined to be short-lived. At the head of their Getic allies was the powerful and ambitious Burebista, "the greatest and most important of the kings of Thrace," as a contemporary inscription calls him; to him they now became subject. During the disturbances Histria must have been so seriously damaged as to need complete rebuilding, for a decree of sometime after 50 B.C. refers to its "second founding." We have seen how Burebista's interests seemed best served by an alliance with Pompey against Caesar in Rome's civil war of 49–45 B.C., and how, after Pompey's defeat and murder, in 48, the victorious Caesar planned a campaign to remove Burebista once and for all. But the assassination of both in 44 postponed hostilities.

Burebista's tribal alliance broke up, as we saw, and the Pontic cities regained their independence. They continued to bet on the wrong horse: there was a Geto-Dacian contingent with the Caesar-murderers Brutus and Cassius when they were defeated at Philippi in 42 B.C. Since Dobruja continued to be restless, a Roman army commanded, in the name of Caesar's heir Octavian, by M. Licinius Crassus, grandson of the millionnaire, crushed all resistance there, recovering the battle-standards lost by Antonius in 61; Crassus celebrated a triumph in Rome in 27 B.C. Rome controlled Dobruja under Quisling native chiefs, but Histria, Tomis, and Callatis were left nominally free under Roman protection. In the year of Crassus's triumph, the Roman Senate saluted Octavian as Augustus; his generals Cn. Cornelius Lentulus and Sex. Aelius Catus (consul in A.D. 4) suppressed native revolts; we have seen the archaeological evidence for the latter's destruction of native towns in Muntenia; the contemporary Greek geographer Strabo records how Catus deported fifty thousand Getae across the Danube into Thrace.

At this point we gain a precious eyewitness of conditions in Dobruja in the early years of the Christian era. In A.D. 9 there arrived in Tomis—probably selected as the most important of the Pontic cities under Roman protection—the Roman poet Ovid, exiled for alleged subversion. He lived in Tomis until his death in 17, describing his life there in nine books of pathetic verse-letters home, written at the rate of almost one a month. Of course he exaggerates, his aim being to evoke pity and hence recall. We must therefore discount his tales of perpetual Arctic conditions, of Dobruja as a treeless, vineless tundra, of the natives as without exception *hirsuti, intonsi, pelliti, crudi, feri, saevi, inhumani*—hairy, unshorn, clad in skins, crude, wild, savage, uncultured; some of them spoke Greek and became his friends. Ovid learned Getic and wrote poetry in the language; he greets a Thracian prince as a fellow poet. The Tomitani elected the Roman poet one of their public works commissioners. His evidence makes it clear that one met Getans in the streets of Tomis and that they were at least partially Hellenized.

But for our purpose Ovid's most interesting testimony is that Tomis, at least in the early years of his exile, lived in constant—or, allowing for exaggeration, intermittent—fear of barbarian attack, especially in winter, when, as we saw, he reports that the enemy would cross the Danube on the ice and fire their deadly poisoned arrows within bowshot of the town walls. In the spring, Ovid writes, no plowman would drive a furrow unless he was armed, and the poet himself—a pathetic picture—had to put a helmet on his gray head and join the Tomitani in guard duty. A pre-Ovidian Greek inscription from Tomis mentions a special militia on day and night duty to deal with such emergencies. Tomis was not the only city menaced: Ovid mentions also Aegyssus and Troesmis, now Tulcea and Iglița (fig. 5.1). The former was attacked in A.D. 12, the latter in 15, but these attacks evoked efficient Roman countermeasures, so that Ovid's latest poems make no mention of further barbarian raids. He died peacefully in Tomis in 17; today the main square of Constanța is named for him, and a nineteenth-century bronze statue of him (fig. 6.2.)—by an Italian—rises in its midst.

6.2. Constanța, Ovid statue

Augustus's stepson and successor, Tiberius, determined to put an end to barbarian unrest. A contemporary Roman historian, Velleius Paterculus, describes the perilous situation a little farther west: "Roman citizens overpowered, traders massacred, a large detachment of veterans, stationed in a region most remote from the commander, exterminated to a man . . . everywhere wholesale devastation by fire and sword." Tiberius's solution was to lean no longer upon the broken reed of Thracian mercenaries, but to set Dobruja up as a Roman province, defended by Roman legions. He did this early in his reign, probably in A.D. 15. The province was called Moesia; it extended beyond the bounds of present-day Romania, where it does not concern us, but of its three legions, one was stationed in Dobruja, at Troesmis. The system worked: after the crushing of a native revolt in the region, in A.D. 26, peace lasted for over forty years. It was Tiberius's general C. Poppaeus Sabinus, the grandfather of the notorious red-haired wife of the future emperor Nero, who crushed the revolt of 26; he ruled the province for twenty years (15–35). From 57 to 67 of Nero's reign the governor of Moesia was Ti. Plautius Silvanus Aelianus, about whom we know a good deal from an inscription found by his family mausoleum near Tibur, modern Tivoli, fifteen miles east of Rome. The inscription records that he transplanted to Moesia—and forced to pay tribute—more than one hundred thousand Transdanubians with their wives and children, chiefs and kings. With only a fraction of his army he nipped in the bud a Sarmatian uprising. Kings hitherto unknown or hostile to the Roman people he brought to the Danube frontier to pay homage to the Roman battle-standards; from other kings he took hostages, as a guarantee of peace, which he strengthened and advanced; he was the first to add to the grain supply of the Roman people a great quantity of Moesian wheat, and he boasts that he made the Black Sea in effect a Roman lake.

Archaeological evidence is scanty in Dobruja for the first two hundred years or so of Roman rule. Tomis and Callatis are, as we saw, built over; at Histria and along the Danube excavation has seldom reached the levels of the early principate. But at Noviodunum (now Isaccea), a dozen miles west of the Danube delta, salvage archaeology, undertaken as the remains were sliding into the river, revealed 250 meters of the towered north wall of the fort, whose earliest phase, dated by coins, may be Neronian. Under the following Flavian dynasty, and perhaps earlier, it was an important base of the Roman Danube river fleet.

The main base of the Flavian fleet was Bărboşi, four miles south-west of Galaţi, where the course of the Danube turns from north to east. Galaţi today is the seat of an important Romanian navy yard. At Bărboşi, excavation has established that the Romans built, per-haps under the Flavian emperor Domitian (81–96) an earthwork camp over the original Geto-Dacian settlement mentioned at the end of chapter 3. In Domitian's reign, it will be recalled, Daco-Getan power revived under the redoubtable Decebalus. In the second year (86) of Domitian's war against Decebalus (85–89), the emperor split Moesia into two provinces, Inferior (the lower Danube) and Superior (the upper, outside the boundaries of present-day Ro-mania). Inferior was created presumably to provide a legionary head-quarters closer to the scene of operations against Decebalus, who was ravaging Dobruja and had already, farther west at Tapae, killed one Roman general, Cornelius Fuscus, and massacred his army, a disaster compared by a modern Romanian historian to the catastrophic loss of Quintilius Varus and three whole legions in the Teutoburg Forest in Germany seventy-six years before.[1] A new general, Tettius Julianus, by stern discipline whipped the demoralized legions into shape, and beat Decebalus, again at Tapae, in 88. The peace terms were sensible from Domitian's point of view: they made Decebalus nominally a satellite prince and kept him ostensibly quiet for a dozen years. To a hard-headed Roman, paying a native chief protection-money now seemed, three-quarters of a century after Tiberius, as cheap as ex-panding an expensive all-Roman army of occupation. But we saw how Decebalus used Roman engineers and deserters to build the power with which he was to face Trajan. For fifteen years before Domitian's war with Decebalus, and for the dozen years after it, until Trajan, Romanization in Dobruja proceeded apace. Veterans settled as colonists in villae rusticae; Histria, Tomis, and Callatis prospered, with their own mint, and their own coalition, showing their loyalty to Rome by honoring the imperial cult, and celebrating games in honor of the Caesars. Tomis did good business as a trans-

1. See MacKendrick, *Romans on the Rhine*, pp. 77–81.

shipment point for goods from the motherland, bound for the Danube and beyond, and though Histria's harbor silted up, from about A.D. 49 the Romans guaranteed her—in a surviving inscription —the tax-free enjoyment of fishing rights in the Danube delta. Callatis exploited her fertile hinterland in a flourishing grain trade.

We have already discussed Trajan's Dobruja campaign in his First Dacian War. His experience there made it clear to him that Dobruja was an invasion corridor and had to be controlled. Within eyeshot of his monument at Adamclisi, just to the south, he established veterans at Tropaeum Traiani, which grew, as we shall see in the next chapter, to be a prosperous walled city with sumptuous buildings, covering twenty-four acres. North of it, along the Danube, he built a string of forts, the Danube limes: Axiopolis, Capidava, Carsium (for which there is evidence as early as 103), Cius, Troesmis, Arrubium (fig. 5.1), linking up with the naval base at Bărboşi, which he enlarged in 112. Most of the archaeological evidence for these forts belongs to a later period, to a remarkable flowering of Dobruja from Constantine (306–37) to Justinian (527–65), which testifies to the noteworthy vitality of the Eastern empire while the West was in full decline, and tottering to its fall. This evidence will be discussed in the next chapter.

Meanwhile, what of the Trajanic limes? Much of the evidence, e.g., at Axiopolis, comes from inscribed stones or stamped tiles reused in later walls. At Capidava, later very important, the only trace of the Trajanic camp is a doorsill and part of a tower incorporated into the massive Constantinian fortification-wall. We know that Carsium (now Hîrşova) was built over an important Geto-Greek settlement whose location, opposite the mouth of the Ialomiţa River, made it the logical diffusion point for Greek goods bound for the Muntenian and Dacian hinterland. Much of the Roman evidence comes from monuments reused in the medieval castle. Twenty-five miles to the southeast, Ulmetum (Pantelimon de Sus) was important both to strategy and to economics, lying as it did at the junction of the east-west road from Histria to the Danube, and the north-south route through the center of Dobruja, down which so many barbarian hordes would pass if it were not protected. Here the Roman fort is Trajanic. At Troesmis, later also very important, we know from a building inscription that Trajan stationed a legion (V Macedonica)

6.3. Carsium, bronze parade helmet

as early as 112. And that, for the time being, is all, archaeologically speaking. Historically, the important point to notice is that Trajan's Danube limes gave to Dobruja the longest period of security it had ever known or was to know until modern times.

Hadrian, the philhellene peacemaker, had no intention of abandoning Dobruja. He knew well its strategic importance and its cultural (Hellenic) prestige, having commanded the Fifth Macedonian Legion under Domitian and fought with distinction in both Dacian wars, including Trajan's Dobruja campaign. He visited Dobruja twice, in 118, and in 123–24. Inscriptions in his honor have turned up in Histria, Troesmis, and Tomis. From this last, an inscription in Latin—rare in Dobruja—metamorphoses the town's Greek *boulê* and *demos* into *Senatus Populusque Tomanitorum*. His policy was twofold: he prevented Sarmatian raids by giving a higher subsidy; and he recruited troops locally, thus insuring their loyalty (they were defending their own hearths and homes), hastening their Romanization, and motivating the building of canabae near the camps. The time was still distant when the barbarians in the Roman army would feel more loyalty to their blood brothers in the enemy lines than to their Roman paymasters. During the Hadrianic *pax Romana,* the army held war games rather than fighting in earnest. The evidence is the face mask of a bronze parade helmet from Carsium (fig. 6.3).[2]

2. Cf. ibid., fig. 4.18, a similar mask from Straubing in Bavaria.

The face is that of an idealized young man in the prime of life, with thick curly hair, in which he wears a crown of laurel fastened with a rosette. Such helmets, the products of Italian workshops, turn up frequently in or near Roman camps of the second Christian century. Two others were discovered in 1960 at Ostrov, south of the Danube, but still in Romania: Ostrov was the necropolis of the Roman camp of Durostorum (now Silistra, in Bulgaria). These helmets, too, were made in Italy, perhaps somewhat later than the one from Carsium; the fact that they were found in graves shows that officers could keep them after retirement.

The reign of Hadrian's successor, Antoninus Pius, marks the apogee of prosperity and Romanization in Dobruja. Histria had sumptuous buildings, of which some marble architraves remain; Tomis began to call itself "the metropolis of the Euxine" (Black Sea), and built a portico and port-works. Capidava became a customs station; canabae flourished at Troesmis; the naval station at Bărboşi continued active. The unusual number of milestones from this reign shows that the first Antonine emperor was especially interested in keeping the roads in repair. Even the complaints show that the natives had access to the governor and that grievances were remedied. In an interesting inscription from rural Scaptopara near Histria, the villagers complain—like the colonists just before the American Revolution—of excessive exactions, quartering of troops upon them, the expense of entertaining the many official missions (they were on a main military road, which did not turn out to be, for them, an unmixed blessing). Appended to the complaint, which is in Greek, is the governor's reply, in Latin, granting them relief. They carved it in stone and posted it on the highway for the instruction of passing bureaucrats, military or civilian.

This reign yields a piece of archaeological evidence from Dinogetia (Garvăn), a site destined to become much more important later. This is a house, outside the Roman walls, which yielded pottery both local and Roman, thus showing that the native population was not deported, but lived in the canabae adjoining the camp.

Antoninus Pius's successor, Marcus Aurelius (161–80), was forced in 167, by the exigencies of his Marcomannic War, to make the already mentioned transfer of the Fifth Macedonian Legion from Troesmis to Potaissa, leaving only a token force in Dobruja. Troesmis became a civil center, a municipium, and so did Tropacum Traiani. Seizing their opportunity, the Costoboci, from northern Transylvania, swept through Dobruja (170) on their marauding way to Greece, into which they penetrated as far as the holy city of Eleusis, west of Athens. Late learners, the citizens of Tomis and Callatis reinforced their walls. Once the Marcomanni were beaten, Marcus deported twelve thousand free Dacians into Dobruja, repaired the military roads, and reestablished order.

Thanks to an efficient army and civil service, Dobruja did not lose as much as might have been expected under the reign of Marcus Aurelius's son Commodus, well described by a modern Romanian historian as "vain, prideful, uneducable, cruel, petty, depraved, soft, dilettante." Army and navy detachments were kept at Troesmis and Bărboşi, road building continued, and inscriptions in honor of the imperial monster at Tropaeum Traiani, Capidava, Callatis, and Ulmetum show that absolute monarchy was not repugnant to the subjects of the empire in the east. But after his assassination they damned his memory in the usual time-servers' way, by chiseling his name out of the inscriptions.

Under the Severan dynasty (193–235), Dobruja, behind the strong defense of the Danube limes, continued peaceful and prosperous. The march of Romanization is indicated by the impressive number and wide distribution of dedicatory inscriptions to the dynasty: at Tropaeum Traiani, Axiopolis, Capidava, Ulmetum, Troesmis, Arrubium, and the three Greek cities. Septimius Severus passed through Dobruja on his way back from Parthia, probably in 202. He was the first emperor to legalize marriage between soldiers and local women; he permitted the troops to live off base, in the canabae, and to cultivate plots of land nearby. If the husband was a Roman citizen, so were his children; if he was not, he and his children gained citizenship on his discharge. The natural results were three: Romanization spread yet further, and the provincial armies became more sedentary and more regional. Probably in this reign was buried a unique find from a tumulus in 2 Mai, a village just south of Callatis. It shows the persistence of native customs: the remains of a war chariot, with the skeletons of two horses, and their harness: hubcap rings in iron, guide-lines for the reins and a decorative lion's-head plaque in bronze, plus the bottom support and the seat-back braces of the chariot itself. Under Septimius we have evidence of building activity in Tomis: a block from what must have been a very large building—the block is thirteen feet long—bearing a dedication to the emperor in both Greek and Latin, in which this North African is supplied, as he often was, with a fictitious family tree making Nerva his great-great-great grandfather, and continuing, as though in a direct line of descent, through Trajan, Hadrian, Antoninus Pius, and Marcus Aurelius, who is recorded as his father. Obviously the Tomitani thought such bare-faced flattery good insurance. It was; they survived.

A decree of Septimius's villainous son, the fratricide Caracalla, in 212, included Dobrujan communities in an empire-wide grant of Roman citizenship. No generosity was involved; simply a desire to broaden the tax base. An immediately observable result is the increase of bad Latin in Dobrujan inscriptions. These are, in both languages, more fulsome than ever, according to the custom of the time. One would never guess what a monster Caracalla was from references to him at Histria as "invincible," or "lord over land and sea." As absolutism increases, so do the superlatives: Histria styles herself "most glorious." Road maps and itineraries of the period show that the military highway along the right bank of the Danube was kept up, passing through Axiopolis, Capidava, Carsium, Cius, Dinogetia, Arrubium, Noviodunum, and Salsovia (now Mahmudia). An unusual source preserves the evidence for a coast road traveled at this period through the Black Sea port towns: it is a leather shield-cover, from Dura-Europus, far away on the Euphrates, on which are written in Greek the names of the towns through which the owner has traveled on campaign, each marked with the symbol of a tower represented as made of squared stones.

Caracalla was assassinated in 217. Though his successor, Macrinus, lasted only two months, Histria managed to pass decrees in his honor, of which two survive.

The next Severan emperor was Caracalla's nephew, the bizarre and effeminate teenager Elagabalus (217–22); he was only fourteen at his accession. His fanaticism was centered in Oriental, especially Syrian, cults: the evidence for these increases markedly in his reign.

Under the last Severan, the good but bland Severus Alexander (222–35), the troops in Dobruja were given land, which tied them to the province and insured their loyalty, but virtually reduced them to the status of serfs. Histria, as usual, honored the emperor with inscriptions. Tomis, with a blunter recognition of the real locus of power, made a dedication to his mother, Julia Mammaea: the thirteen-year-old Alexander was firmly under her thumb. Boundary stones from Ulmetum and Capidava attest the continuation of farm life there in this reign: they are dated by the consuls of 229, one of whom was the historian Dio Cassius, who is one of our chief literary sources for the period. Perhaps the future Emperor Decius was governor of Moesia Inferior under Alexander.

There follows a period of decadence for Dobruja, under the military anarchy: a 50-year span (235–84), which saw twenty-four emperors rise and fall—more than in the previous 262 years since the Senate proclaimed Octavian Augustus in 27 B.C. It was a time of plague, depopulation, famine, social cleavage, and invasion—and Dobruja was directly in its path. The first emperor of this sad period, Maximinus, called the Thracian (235–38), was a native of Moesia, a giant of a man, nearly eight feet tall, who consumed forty pounds of meat a day, and seven gallons of wine; he daily collected his own sweat, which amounted to a quart and a half. In his youth he had been a shepherd; he owed his preferment to Septimius Severus. He spoke Latin with a Thracian accent. These monstrosities of course did not prevent Histria, Capidava, and Ulmetum from saluting him in honorific decrees: Histria called him "lord of land and sea, and of all mankind." A milestone from Ibida, now Slava Rusă (fig. 2.1), halfway between Histria and Troesmis, shows that the central Dobruja military highway was repaired during his reign. Also from Ibida, but rather earlier in date, comes a tombstone with a relief of the she-wolf suckling Romulus and Remus (fig. 6.4); like the one from Alba Iulia (fig. 5.9), it is a symbol of Romanization. A sign of impoverishment appears in the reduced circulation of coinage: only Tomis and Callatis minted money, and it was only bronze.

In the single year 238, the empire had seven rulers in succession. When the tumult and the shouting died, the survivor was the thirteen-year-old Gordian III (238–44) during whose reign the Carpi invaded Dobruja, taking the recently repaired central road, and sparing the coastal cities. A Histrian inscription, formerly thought to refer to warfare ([be]LLVM) there, is now more prosaically re-

6.4. Ibida, wolf and twins, relief

6.5. Tomis, priestess of Isis

stored as referring to rebuilding a market ([mace]LLVM). Tomis
built a temple to Isis. A sculptured head of a priestess of the goddess, found there (fig. 6.5), is said to represent Gordian's wife, Furia
Sabinia Tranquillina, daughter of his praetorian prefect. Callatis
honored them both. Altars to Gordian at Tropaeum Traiani and
Ulmetum, and a milestone at Carsium prove that the Carpi spared
all three places. The river fleet was still in being, called "Gordiana,"
and under the command of a freed slave.

A Bedouin chief, Philip the Arab, whom Gordian made his praetorian prefect, arranged his murder and took over the throne. In his
reign (244–49) was celebrated (247) the thousandth anniversary of
the founding of Rome, but Dobruja had little cause for rejoicing.
The burying of numerous coin hoards is evidence of troubled times:
in 248 the Goths, angry at the suppression of their subsidy, invaded
Moesia, thirty thousand strong. Philip was killed in battle at Verona
in 249. His successor, Decius, fell, too, in a blitzkrieg (251), along
with his eldest son. Decius was the first Roman emperor to fall before the barbarians. His successor, Trebonianus Gallus (251–53),
bribed the Goths to retire, with their booty and prisoners, into
Muntenia and Moldavia, thus driving a permanent wedge between
Dobruja and Dacia.

The Romans had by now lost their reputation for invincibility.
Dobruja became a *via gentium*—a veritable highway for barbarians
to sweep through. The Goths invaded again, along with the Carpi,
in 253. The reign of Valerian (253–60) exhibits a regular rash of
invasions and usurpers, along with persecutions of Christians, who
were held responsible, as mockers of the pagan gods, for a chronic
plague. But a milestone from Carsium gives a clue that the Danube
limes was consolidated, and the future Emperor Aurelian beat back a
land attack of barbarians in Dobruja.

Valerian's son Gallienus (260–68) took bloody vengeance on
Dobruja for collaboration with usurpers. One of these, Regalianus,
claimed descent from Decebalus himself. In 263 the Sarmatians invaded the Propontis and Asia Minor, apparently bypassing Histria
and Tomis, but the whole southwest quarter of Callatis, outside the
walls, perished by fire at this time; in one of the houses was found a
hoard of nine thousand coins, and the skeleton of its owner, burned
to death while trying to save his treasure. Histria, so long spared, was

6.6. Histria, late wall, columns in reuse

finally sacked, probably in 267. After the fact, a wall was built in great haste across the peninsula from north to south (fig. 2.2, no. 7), using, in an understandably panic-stricken way, whatever stone material was at hand: imperial decrees, theater seats, gravestones, religious and secular sculpture, temple architraves and columns. Figure 6.6 shows columns in reuse in the bottom course of the wall.

The surname of Claudius II (268–70) was Gothicus. He earned it by a decisive defeat of the Goths at Naissus, far to the west, in Moesia Superior (now Niš, Yugoslavia). But before that, a massive sea migration of Goths, 320,000 of them, we are told, in two thousand ships, hit Tomis. Thanks to its strong walls and independent water supply (the underground conduits for which excavation has revealed), it held out, but the citizens' panic is betrayed by the discovery, near the railway station, of a cache of twenty-four statues (figs. 6.7–8) buried for safekeeping at the time of the Gothic invasion. The head of the priestess-empress, figure 6.5, lies face down at the lower left; other pieces will be illustrated and described in greater detail in the last chapter.

6.7. Constanța, sculpture cache, as found

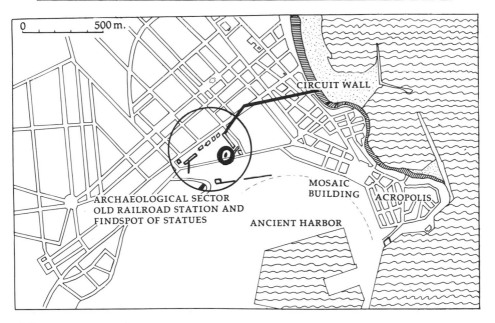

6.8. Constanţa, plan

And so we come to Aurelian (270–75). We have seen how his
"abandonment" of Dacia meant simply the orderly withdrawal of the
army, the civil service, and the timid rich. Dobruja he did not
abandon at all: it continued a part of the Roman Empire for over
350 years, though the naval base at Bărboşi appears to have been
given up. Aurelian beat the Carpi, settling some of them in the
canabae of Carsium. Tropaeum Traiani honored him (in bad Latin,
with misspellings and mistakes in gender); Callatis hailed him
RESTITVTOR PATRIAE—"restorer of the fatherland." But Dobruja had
suffered terribly, and the withdrawal of troops from Dacia left it
dangerously open to attack. Especially outside the walled towns, the
Dobrujans were the victims of epidemic, economic stagnation,
rapacious troops, and greedy tax-gatherers. The evidence is the
poverty of the archaeological remains of the late third century: few
if any inscriptions, coins, new buildings, or art (the buried sculpture
at Tomis is all from an earlier period). Recovery would have to wait

for a generation. It came with Constantine (306–37) and the revival
of the Danube limes, a story to be told in the next chapter.

Meanwhile, as we review 260 years of Dobrujan history, from the
founding of the province of Moesia in 15 to the death of Aurelian in
275, let us remember that at least half those years were years of
peace. In Moesia, as in Dacia, Roman rule stimulated agriculture and
commerce, encouraged city life, guaranteed municipal autonomy,
raised the rural standard of living, and promoted a higher level of
culture. In Moesia, as in Dacia, Roman rule had also its seamy side:
occasional brutality, exploitation, extortion. But, as in Dacia, the
good outweighs the bad. The Roman peace made possible the trans-
mission of Greek culture, the reduction of slavery (fewer war captives), the reinvigorating of Greek art. Roman administration opened
careers to provincial talent. The Romans, themselves descended from
a hardy race of farmers, had particular success with the Dobrujan
peasantry. The Geto-Dacian spirit of independence was so strong
that it was nearly sixty years from the death of Burebista before
Dobruja could be set up as a province, but when it was, it passed as
a legitimate successor to Burebista's rule, though the Roman administration at its top levels was also a Latin enclave in a Geto-Greek
land. Here, as in Dacia, Rome showed, at least until the Severan
dynasty, her old tradition of order, practicality, logic, correctness,
tolerance, moderation, adaptability. Here as elsewhere, Rome first
conquered, then assimilated, manifesting, in her best days in Dobruja,
the two qualities that a Domitianic poet called the twin props of empire: *virtus belli et sapientia pacis*—competence in war, wisdom in
peace.

7. DACIA AND MOESIA
DURING THE LATE EMPIRE

To the archaeologist more familiar with the Western empire, one of the most extraordinary things about the ancient history of Romania is how long it lasts. In Dacia, the bridgeheads at Drobeta and Sucidava were still in existence in the reign of Justinian (527–65); in Dobruja, Histria endured into that of Heraclius (610–41), by which time the Roman Empire in the West had been over for 135 years. The central point of difference is that in the East the central administration did not break down, as is proved by Justinian's Code and his chain of fortresses along the Danube, the plans for which were in all probability drawn up in Constantinople.

In Dacia, the withdrawal of the imperial bureaucracy from all but the bridgeheads at Drobeta and Sucidava means that official documentation is scanty or nonexistent. But excavation of settlements and cemeteries vouches for the continuance of the native population, and coins and milestones show that economic life and traffic went on in the old Roman towns, now given over to the Dacians. At Dierna, there are coins until the reign of Justinian; at Apulum and Porolissum, to Theodosius I (379–95); Romula yields a milestone of 328, during the reign of Constantine (306–37). The coins at Napoca last till the reign of Theodosius II (408–50); a treasure found at nearby Someşeni in 1963 is probably East Gothic, the property of a Christian German princess, who buried it in the third quarter of the fifth century, in the troubled times after the death of Attila the Hun. The finds, all of gold, include a twisted chain, pendants set with garnets, a filigree pectoral, a massive belt buckle, bracelets, and rings.

At Drobeta, Constantine rebuilt the Trajanic camp, on the same footings but with only one gate (fig. 7.1). Just within the wall, postholes suggest that there were wooden casemates, whose flat roofs

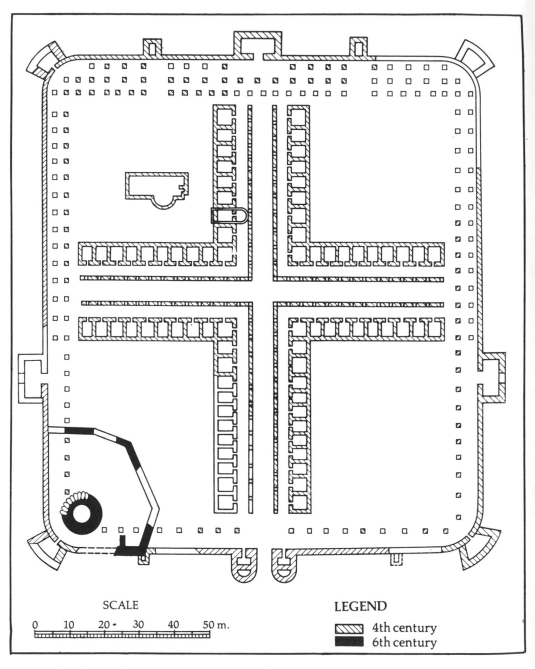

SCALE

0   10   20 ·   30   40   50 m.

LEGEND

4th century
6th century

7.1. Drobeta, Constantinian camp, plan

served as artillery platforms. The barracks were arranged in a cruciform plan, with eighty-four rooms, each opening on an arcaded
portico. Attila destroyed this camp in the mid-fifth century. Justinian
rebuilt it in the sixth, renaming it after his wife, the notorious actress
Theodora. The tower in the southwest corner of the plan belongs to
this phase; it incorporates in its fabric nine gravestones from the pre-
Constantinian period, including one of a young army doctor who
doubled as a town councilor, and died at the age of twenty-three.

Sucidava also got a new lease on life under Constantine. In 328 he
built a bridge across the Danube here, a mile and a half long.[1] The
footings of its north portal are visible, west of the citadel Constantine built to protect it (fig. 5.6). In 1933 divers found three of
its piers in midstream; at low water in the summer of 1971 swirls
in the current indicated its location. The bridge lasted less than forty
years: the Emperor Valens was unable to use it for his expedition
north of the Danube against the Goths in 367. But floods and ice
were more likely agents of its destruction than barbarians, for the
citadel continued in use until Attila destroyed it in 447. It is triangular in plan, and protected by a ditch. Its two impressive surviving walls—the Danube has eroded the third side—measure 525 and
426 feet, were originally thirteen to twenty feet high, and have seven
towers, which could be used as artillery platforms. The original entrance was on the south; a postern in the third tower from the south
gave access to the town, across the moat, which must have been
spanned by a light demountable wooden bridge. In the masonry of
the wall, the courses of squared stone are interrupted by three layers
of bricks: the technique, called *opus mixtum* or *opus listatum,* is
characteristic of Constantine's time. The guard was housed in all the
towers except one, where the discovery of two feet of carbonized
grain on the floor show that it was used for storage. Just inside the
perimeter, postholes like those at Drobeta held the supports for a
wall-walk. Within the citadel, the barracks were of wood: Attila's
sack left a level of wood-ash twenty inches thick. Three coin hoards
found within the walls date from Constantine to Theodosius II

1. He built another, a pontoon bridge, in the same year, between Trans-
marisca (fig. 5.1) and Constantiniana Daphne on the north bank. The Emperor Valens also built one there in 367 to facilitate his expedition against the
Goths, and yet another at Noviodunum.

(408–50). Finds of farm tools and a double flute show what the soldiers did with their spare time; a bronze frying pan, pathetically mended with copper and iron patches, suggests shortage both of metals and of skills.

After the sack by Attila, the citadel was unoccupied for nearly a hundred years, until Justinian reactivated it. Two interesting structures mark this phase. The first is an apsidal building, measuring 72 by 33 feet, which the discovery of Christian symbols identifies as a basilica-church, the earliest yet found north of the Danube. In the Byzantine Empire, Orthodox Christianity was the established church: Justinian's revitalizing of it dates from 535. The basilica is oriented east and west, with the altar in the east, as was—and is—canonical. The footings for the lectern are visible in the floor; beneath it were found three coffins, one bearing the sign of the cross. Other finds were a clay lamp with a cruciform handle, and an amphora—with a capacity of sixteen gallons—for the communion wine, painted in Greek with the words "Mary, the mother of Christ the son of God." Two rooms were added later on the south to serve as the vestry. The latest coins are dated 596–97, in the reign of the Emperor Maurice (582–602), when the Avars and Slavs sacked the citadel.

The other interesting structure of this late phase of the citadel has been christened by its excavator, Professor Dumitru Tudor of the University of Bucharest, the "Secret Spring." Since there is no natural water within the citadel, the defenders dug a tunnel under the south wall to a spring outside. Such tunnels are known from Bronze Age Mycenae, Tiryns, and Athens,[2] but this is claimed as unique in the Byzantine or Roman world. The builders first dug sixteen feet straight down—the water-carriers would negotiate this stretch by ladder—then built a vaulted ramp eighty-five feet long, sloping downward under the south wall of the citadel with steps at intervals to the spring. At the level of Danube high water, an outlet, too small for invaders to crawl through, was placed to relieve pressure on the ramp walls. The last coins suggest that the Avars and Slavs discovered the secret shortly after 596–97. The ramp is still practicable; one lights one's way with votive candles of beeswax; the spring still holds water. The excavation foreman finds it potable; it

2. See MacKendrick, *Greek Stones Speak,* figs. 2.4, 5 and 3.3.

made me, an unwitting martyr to archaeology, deathly ill.

In the disputed territory between Dacia and Moesia a key site is Tîrgşor. As the map (fig. 5.1) shows, there was a Roman auxiliary camp here, but, like its neighbors, it was abandoned under Hadrian. A large, late necropolis (268 graves) shows Sarmatian burials, identified by deliberately deformed skulls, contemporary with Geto-Dacian cremations, identified by pottery, fibulas, and weapons; some of the pottery, decorated with a toothed wheel, is Roman. About one hundred of the cremations belong to the Sîntana de Mureş culture, i.e., to an originally Germanic people who, forced eastward from the Baltic by the Goths, came down from the upper Dnieper into Muntenia in the fourth Christian century. The evidence of the adjoining settlement seems to be that the free Dacians assimilated the others, while maintaining trade relations with potters in the Roman provinces to the south and west.

We turn now to Moesia, where the continuing Roman presence makes the archaeological evidence much richer. The reforms of Diocletian (284–305) changed the name of the province to Scythia Minor, and placed it under the diocese of Thrace. New legions—I Iovia and II Herculea—now did guard duty in the camps, which Diocletian rebuilt or strengthened. The one for which we have the best evidence dating from his reign is Dinogetia (now Bisericuţa, in the township of Garvăn), about five miles southeast of Bărboşi (fig. 5.1), on an easily defensible plateau overlooking what was in antiquity a tributary of the Danube. The evidence for dating is coins, a milestone, a military kiln that produced tiles stamped with the name of Diocletian's Legion I Iovia, and the massive walls themselves (fig. 7.2), ten feet thick, set with fourteen horseshoe-shaped towers, with a single towered gate on the southeast, and a postern in the middle of the west side. The wall was built of all new cut stone (no inscriptions in reuse), in two faces, rubble-filled.

The square building with the four pillars, in the north half of the citadel, was the commandant's headquarters; among the finds in it was a number of clay catapult-balls of various calibers; elsewhere were found spear- and arrowheads, and fragments of a steel breastplate. Immediately east of the headquarters building, with only a narrow alley between, rose a large 92-by-62-foot eight-room dwelling,

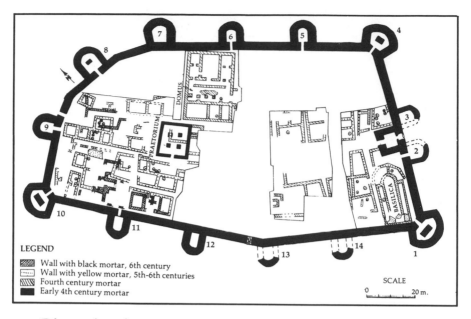

7.2. Dinogetia, plan

7.3. Dinogetia, aristocratic house, reconstruction drawing

with porch, peristyle, and lararium, or shrine of the household gods (fig. 7.3). It was so sumptuous that its excavator, Professor Ion Barnea, has dubbed it "the aristocratic house." Like the rest of the citadel, it was sacked, probably by the Huns in 375, rebuilt under Anastasius I (491–518), and this time survived till the citadel finally fell in 559.

The buildings north and west of the headquarters, and just east of the main gate, must have been storehouses, for large dolia were found in them, such as the Romans used as containers for water, wine, oil, and grain. Other finds included the usual pottery, bronze figurines, and jewelry; slightly less ordinary were farm tools, a gridiron, glassware, and a bronze balance-scale stamped, to guarantee honest weight, with the name of Gerontius, eparch (prefect) of Constantinople—Constantine's New Rome on the Golden Horn, built between 324 and 330. Also of interest is the Christian basilica, tucked into the southeast corner; its apse was frescoed in red, blue, and brown.

Three hundred feet outside the main gate were the baths, noteworthy as containing the best preserved hypocaust in Romania. They belong to the late fourth century: in the sixth, when godliness was apparently more important than cleanliness, one of their rooms was remodeled into a Christian chapel.

Outside the walls to the west were the canabae, inhabited by farmers and fishermen, as finds such as a plowshare and fishhooks prove. Like the citadel garrisons, they fell before the invaders in 559. The revival of the site, and its subsequent history down to the twelfth century, fall outside the scope of this book.

Capidava, originally, as we saw, a Trajanic fort on the Danube limes between Axiopolis and Carsium, was rebuilt in the late third century to hold a detachment of Diocletian's Legio II Herculea. Its massive walls enclosed an area of 417 by 344 feet (fig. 7.4). A nineteenth-century stone quarry ate away its western corner (upper right quadrant on the plan), but enough remains to show that it had a single gate with a single tower, in the east (plan, left center), that the corner towers were quarter-circles, the center ones rectangular, and the intermediate (curtain) towers horseshoe-shaped. The apsidal building and the one adjoining with the two rows of piers (plan, upper left quadrant) were part of the headquarters complex; the re-

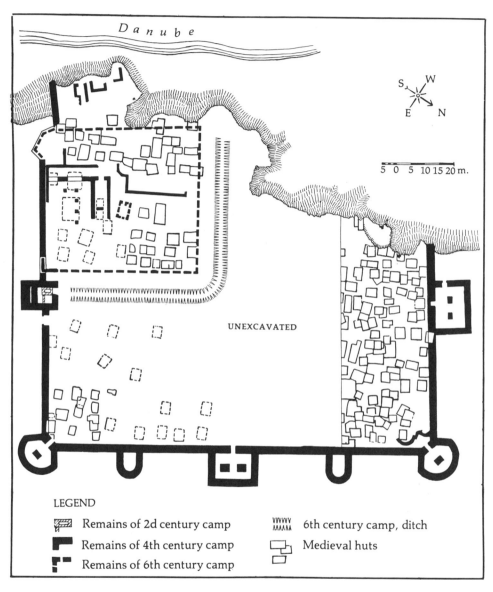

Danube

UNEXCAVATED

5 0 5 10 15 20 m.

LEGEND

▨ Remains of 2d century camp   ⋁⋁⋁⋁⋁⋀⋀⋀⋀⋀ 6th century camp, ditch

◼ Remains of 4th century camp   ⬒ Medieval huts

◖ Remains of 6th century camp

7.4. Capidava, plan

mains on the south, by the Danube (upper left corner) were the
camp baths, built within the walls. Like Dinogetia, this camp was
destroyed by invaders, and rebuilt after 337, under the sons of Constantine the Great. The Constantinian rebuilding was poor, straggly
work, as can be seen in figure 7.5, showing the east tower, where the
large blocks in the lower courses belong to the earlier phase, the
smaller stones to the later. Within can be seen the piers that supported the floor of the tower's second story; at the left edge, one of
the horseshoe-shaped curtain-towers, with the remains of a rectangular one beyond. The Huns destroyed this phase in the late fifth
century; when Justinian rebuilt the camp, it squatted disconsolately
in the south corner of the old walls (within the dotted lines on the
plan), occupying only a quarter of the former area, with the old main
gate blocked. The stones of this phase were robbed to build the
medieval huts that the plan shows crowded all over the excavated
area. Justinian's citadel fell, like Dinogetia, in the early seventh century, to the Avars and Slavs.

Civilian remains include evidence for two local crafts, the potter's
and the stonemason's. For the former, we have a mold for making
terra sigillata, showing Cupids; for the latter, a number of unfinished

7.5. Capidava, east tower

orders, where the relief has been carved, but the inscription not filled in. A pectoral cross in bronze, originally inset with semiprecious stones, bears out literary evidence that Capidava had a bishop. And in the cemetery to the east, a pathetic grave bears witness to the savagery of the barbarian invasions. It contained the skeleton of a female Christian slave with a deformed foot: her collarbone is broken, and her skull bashed in.

Constantine the Great did a great deal of rebuilding in Dobruja. From Tropaeum Traiani we are fortunate enough to have an inscription recording the building of the Constantinian town, precisely dated in 316 by the names of the two praetorian prefects of that year. The inscription was designed to be placed over the east gate, together with a model of Trajan's trophy nearby. It is a dedication to Constantine and his colleague and brother-in-law Licinius, but Licinius fell into disfavor, and his name was chiseled out. The text praises the emperor's valor and foresight, records that the barbarians have everywhere been brought to heel (*edomiti*), and states that the aim of the rebuilding is to assure the defense of the limes. The splendid new town replaced one destroyed by the Goths, probably in 295. Its walls (see plan, fig. 7.6), thirteen feet thick at the base, had twenty-two towers, and enclosed an area of twenty-four acres. The rectangular tower (4 on the plan) was used for storage: dolia were found in it. The town had three gates (1, 5, and 6), of which the east was for pedestrians and the west for vehicles; the south gate was a postern. The *via principalis* (8), from the east gate to the west, is nearly one thousand feet long and fifty feet wide, including the porticoed sidewalks on each side. A drain runs under the center of the roadway. At right angles to it runs the *via forensis* (9), also drained. Instead of sand, its pavement-mortar used the ashes from the Gothic sack. At the junction of the two main streets (12) rose the town's most imposing and handsome building, the Basilica Forensis (fig. 7.7), measuring 184 by 79 feet, divided into a nave and two side aisles by two rows of eighteen columns each. Outside of the building (on the left in the photograph), are the remains of its buttresses, in secondary use as the walls of shops. This is Tropaeum Traiani's only secular basilica, used for law courts and covered markets. The town has no fewer than four others, all Christian: the "simple" basilica (10); the "Byzantine" (11) with

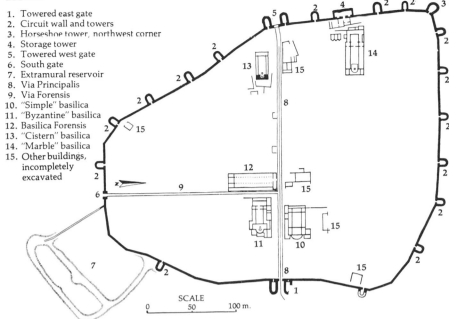

SCALE

0   50   100 m.

7.6. Tropaeum Traiani, plan

7.7. Tropaeum Traiani, Basilica Forensis

transept and crypt; the "cistern," built over the remains of a vaulted reservoir; and the "marble" (14), shown in a reconstruction (fig. 7.8) of its third phase, which dates from Justinian. This must have been the cathedral: the bishop's palace adjoins, as does a triple-apsed baptistry. The final, post-Justinian phase was left unfinished when the final barbarian attack came (after 586, the date of the last coin, of the Emperor Maurice). The evidence is a series of uncompleted capitals, made of marble imported from Greece or Asia Minor, but worked skillfully on the spot. Yet another basilica is known; it was built in the fourth century, in the cemetery north of the town. Tropaeum Traiani, which probably had less than five thousand inhabitants, had in itself no need of five churches: they will have served the rural population as well. Much of the town remains unexcavated, as the plan shows. What has been brought to light is of excellent workmanship, as fine as that in contemporary Tomis or Callatis. There were also four aqueducts, one three miles long, which drained into a large catch basin outside the walls near the south gate (7). All this elegance, all these amenities, fell prey to the barbarians at the end of the sixth or the beginning of the seventh century.

This is probably as good a place as any to discuss Ulmetum, since, though it was, as we saw, a Trajanic foundation, it had a Constantinian phase, to which at least the footings of the walls in figure 7.9 belong; the dimensions of the straight sides are 525 and 460 feet. The two horseshoe-shaped towers flanked the gates; the northwest gate was blocked in a late phase, against the barbarians; the corner towers in the roughly triangular plan are round. The Huns sacked the place in the fifth century; Justinian rebuilt it. The major building was probably the military headquarters; there may have been a Christian chapel in the apse. The Avars burnt it three times; the Emperor Maurice rebuilt it once. The finds include Christian inscriptions, vases, a lamp with the figure of a gladiator, Avar arrowheads, lead-backed mirrors, and combs.

Architecturally, Tomis under Constantine deserved the epithet "most glorious," which she so immodestly applied to herself in inscriptions. She earned it by building an elaborate four-terraced complex (fig. 7.10) southwest of the modern Piaţa Ovidiu, on the steep slope leading down to the commercial harbor. This was discovered in 1959 in the course of construction work in the area. The top

7.8. Tropaeum Traiani, "marble" basilica, reconstruction drawing

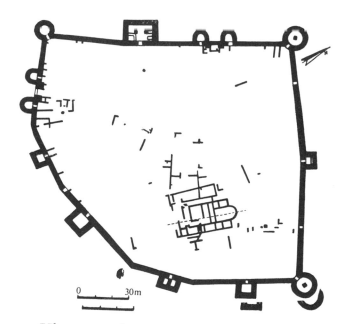

7.9. Ulmetum, plan

level (fig. 7.10, terrace A) could not be excavated because of modern
buildings, but a part of it has been made into a small park where inscriptions from the site are displayed. From here it is a 23-foot drop
to the next and most interesting terrace (B), 328 feet long and 65
feet wide, entirely paved with what is claimed as the largest ancient
mosaic in Europe (two thousand square meters). It is the largest
geometric mosaic; the largest *figured* one is in Grand, a village in
the Vosges.[3] Though the excavators found no evidence that the area
was roofed in antiquity, the mosaic is now protected by a handsome
light and airy modern building. The retaining wall between terraces
A and B was revetted with white and polychrome marble; at thir-
teen-foot intervals were Corinthian pilasters that supported an arcade.
The mosaic itself is made of tesserae in five colors: black, white,
cream, yellow, and pink, set in seventy-four different designs, in
which geometric motifs predominate, though there are also (fig.
7.11) ivy leaves, guilloches, running spirals, *cantharoi* (two-handled
vases), shields, and double axes. The central band of this vast marble
carpet was divided into seven fields, alternately square and round
(fig. 7.11, top), bordered on each side by a strip with rhomboids or
lozenges and framed all the way round by an ivy-leaf design. This
level must have been an attractive gathering-place, an adjunct to
the neighboring agora.

Opening on to terrace C were eleven vaulted rooms, used as warehouses. One of them still bears, carved over the door in Greek, the
name of Hermes, god of trade. In the rooms were found masses of
fallen mosaic, which landed there when an earthquake shattered the
complex in the fifth century. Even more significant finds include 160
amphoras, filled with such commodities as resin, asphalt, paint, and
nails; eight iron anchors, a number of large stone weights; lamps and
coins, including those of Constantius II (324–61), by which the complex is dated. It was perhaps he who gave Tomis a new name, Con-
stantiana, of which Constanţa is a corruption. Level D lay beside the
port, and contained commercial buildings and the outlet of one of
the many drains (cuniculi) with which the subsoil of Constanţa is
honeycombed; they made good shelters in case of barbarian attack.

South of the terrace-complex a suite of rooms labeled in a Greek

3. See MacKendrick, *Roman France*, p. 170.

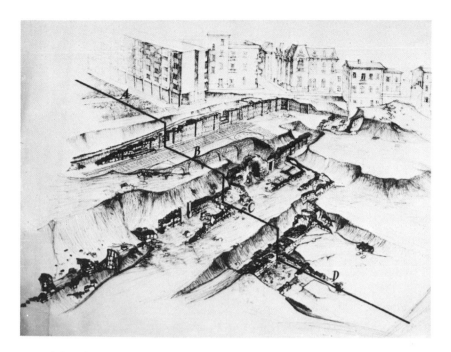

7.10. Tomis, mosaic building, terraces

7.11. Tomis, mosaic, detail

inscription LENTIAPION—a new word in Greek lexicography—were probably baths. Elsewhere in the city building operations have brought to light four Christian basilicas, two near the railway station and two by the port. Across the neck of the Tomis peninsula runs a wall. As it stands, in the midst of the pleasant green lawns of the Archaeological Park, it is a reconstruction of Justinian's time, which includes a multangular tower called "the Butchers'" because a Greek inscription upon it records that the guild of butchers built it at their own expense. Tomis fell late to the Slavic invaders: our last evidence is of 704.

In 369 the emperor Valens made peace with Athanaric, king of the Visigoths. The pact had to be signed on a boat in the middle of the Danube at Noviodunum, since the Visigothic king had sworn never to set foot on Roman soil. Athanaric retired to Pietroasa in Muntenia (Pietroasele on the map, fig. 5.1). To him apparently belonged a gold treasure, an altar set, barbaric in its splendor and extraordinary in its vicissitudes, found there by peasants in 1837. What is left of it, displayed in the treasure room of the new Bucharest museum, consists of twelve pieces, weighing 41½ pounds. I illustrate three of these: first (fig. 7.12), a patera, or sacrificial saucer, ten inches wide ("as big as a mountaineer's hat," said the peasant who found it), representing in relief sixteen Gothic gods with debased classical attributes (e.g., Balder-Apollo, with his lyre), grouped around a central three-dimensional figure of the Earth Mother. Second (fig. 7.13), a twelve-sided cup, its walls, according to its finder, "no thicker than a couple of goose-feathers." It was originally set with precious and semiprecious stones: garnets, carbuncles, emeralds, chrysoprase, rock crystal, pearls, mother-of-pearl, lapis lazuli, turquoise. The reports of the peasant finders—"blue, red, purple and yellow stones," some as big as a millet seed, others as big as a walnut—suggest that there were sapphires, rubies, amethysts, and topazes of various sizes as well: they were all pried out of their settings and either used by children as playthings or sold separately. Third, a huge fibula in the form of a bird's head, "as big as a pigeon" (fig. 7.14). Because there were also three smaller fibulas, the peasants' name for this treasure was "the hen and chickens." There are also on display an eight-sided cup, a neck ring with a Runic inscription, a tray, two necklaces, and a pitcher, which the finder identified correctly as a

7.12. Pietroasa,
gold treasure,
patera

7.13. Pietroasa, gold treasure, twelve-sided cup

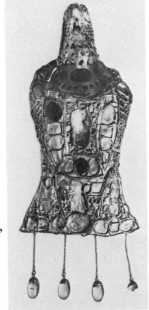

7.14. Pietroasa, gold treasure,
bird's head fibula

holy-water vessel. He knew nothing of gold and precious stones, but he had seen such things as this in church.

The history of the treasure since its discovery is as exotic as the objects themselves. The peasants, who were so poor that they did not recognize gold when they saw it, sold part of the treasure to an Albanian master-mason named Verussi, who was more ignorant—or less pious—than they: he called the holy-water vessel a samovar. He cut up the precious objects with an ax, pried out the inset jewels, and threw them on the farmyard dunghill, where pigs and children rooted for them. The find was treasure trove and legally crown property. The peasants were serfs of the bishop of Buzău, a dozen miles to the northeast. His bailiff having got wind of the discovery, the peasants *gave* him the twelve-sided cup, plus one thousand francs to keep his mouth shut. (They sold a gold chain to the bishop's nephew for a liter of țuica and thirty centimes.) The Albanian, forced by the authorities to disgorge, implicated the peasants, who were flogged and sentenced to a year in prison, where they died. Verussi went on to make a fortune as a state contractor.

The treasure entered the National Museum of Antiquities. In 1867 it was sent to Paris, where the pieces were repaired by a jeweler and displayed at the Exposition in a cabinet whose Second Empire tastelessness is better imagined than described. Then they were taken to the Victoria and Albert Museum in London, where they were photographed; replicas were made of some of the pieces, including the ones illustrated here. Returned to Bucharest amid considerable publicity, they aroused the greed of a young seminarian, who got into the room above them with a skeleton key, sawed a hole in the floor, and let himself down to the treasure, whose case the guards had forgotten to lock. This was in the winter of 1875. The thief flattened the pieces to slip them into his trousers. The twelve-sided cup proving obdurate, he threw it away into the snow, where a professor found it. The police tracked the thief down through his fence: he was given a long prison term and was killed trying to escape. The treasure was "evacuated" to Russia in 1916 and was not returned until 1956. What one sees today, based on the London photographs and replicas, is the work of a restorer from Berlin. If bank-vault security and a military guard are adequate deterrents, the Pietroasa treasure is unlikely to have further exciting adventures.

At Callatis, experts date in the reign of Anastasius I (491–518) a basilica-with-atrium, unique in the Balkans, for it is a type common in Syria, and bespeaks the presence of Syrian Christians doing business in the town. The basilica had a nave, two side aisles, and clerestory (fig. 7.15). The atrium, of which the drawing in figure 7.16 shows a glimpse, had marble columns with rich capitals, in which the Corinthian acanthus motif is combined with rams' heads and eagles holding their prey in their talons. Bits of the marble chancel-rail also came to light: their ornamentation is Christian crosses.

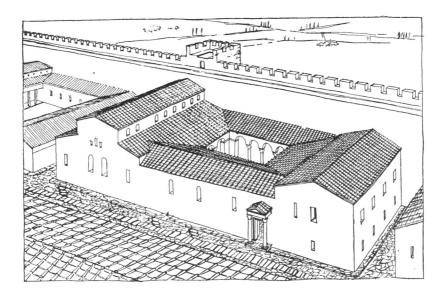

7.15. Callatis,
       "Syrian" basilica,
       reconstruction
       drawing

7.16. Callatis,
       "Syrian" basilica,
       view into atrium,
       reconstruction
       drawing

Justinian's reign saw much building activity in Dobruja; for example, at Troesmis, now Igliţa (fig. 5.1). Troesmis was, as we saw, a Trajanic military foundation, which was made a municipium probably under the Antonines. Two sites have been excavated here, under difficulties that will be described below. The westernmost, about which very little has been published, is described as an isosceles trapezoid, measuring 328 by 492 feet, on a promontory with steep slopes on three sides. About the eastern citadel we know more. It was excavated in the last century, under extreme difficulties. In 1860, the Turkish pasha of Tulcea issued a *firman,* or permission to exploit, to a French engineer, Desiré More, who used the ruins as a quarry. His report places the blame for vandalism on the Turks, who, he says, destroyed inscriptions, sold ancient stones for building materials, burned his buildings, robbed his men, plotted to murder him, and shot off his right thumb. In spite of these difficulties, he claimed that his finds, reported in Vienna, made Troesmis a Mecca for tourists. His successors (1865), Ambroise Baudry and Gaston Boissière, were more scientific; it is on their report of their excavations of the east citadel that the following description is based.

The citadel measured 476 by 394 feet; its site sloped steeply down on all sides except the north (fig. 7.17). The main gate (1) was on the west side. It opened on to a semicircular piazza, with a monumental arch (2) giving on a main west-east street, which divided the citadel into two unequal parts. The south half was military, centering on a Place d'Armes (3), with a tribunal (4) in the center. West of the tribunal, barracks (5–7) were arranged in the form of a U, with a portico, as at Justinian's Drobeta, in front of the central block. Centered on the east side of the Place d'Armes was a Christian basilica (8), its location symbolizing the close connection in Justinian's reign between the orthodox church militant and the army.

The north side of the citadel was the seat of the bishop, and the headquarters of the civilian governor. Number 11, another basilica, with adjacent atrium (12) and council house (13) must have been the cathedral, and number 14 the governor's audience-chamber, with his council house adjoining. Baudry and Boissière identified number 16 as the commandant's headquarters, surrounded on three sides by barracks for his personal bodyguard. Numbers 17 and 18, flanking the main gate, may have been guardhouses; number 19, in the south-

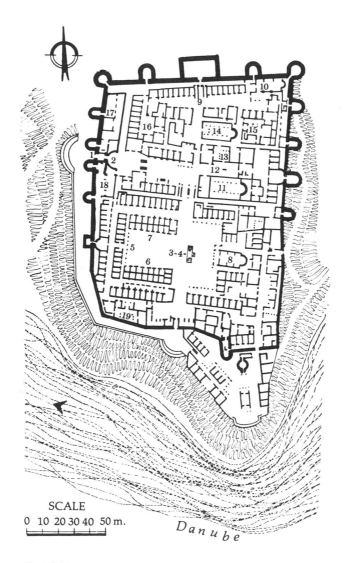

SCALE
0 10 20 30 40 50 m.

Danube

LEGEND

1. Main gate
2. Monumental arch
3-4. Place d'Armes, tribunal
5-7. Barracks
8. Basilica
9-10. Buildings of unknown purpose
11. Bishop's basilica
12. Atrium
13. Council hall (?)
14. Governor's palace
15. Governor's council hall (?)
16. Commandant's HQ, surrounded by barracks
17-18. Guardhouses
19. Officers' quarters or hospital

7.17. Troesmis, plan

west corner, was either officers' quarters or a hospital. The plan
shows Justinian's architect's symmetrical mastery of the space avail-
able: the dominance of the basilicas—and hence of the Christian
church—the complexes so neatly fitted against the circuit walls, the
combination of spaciousness in the Place d'Armes with economy in
the barracks plan, and the provision of separate but equal facilities
for the military, civilian, and ecclesiastical functions of the citadel
within the remarkably small space of a little over four acres. Before
the barbarian threat of Byzantine emperors may have had to retrench,
but here they did it magnificently.

At Axiopolis there are two overlapping forts of our period (fig.
7.18). The coffin-shaped one to the right is the older, Constantinian.
A porticoed street ran from gate to gate, and there was a guardhouse
by its southeast entrance. Later, under Justinian, the fort to the left
was built: two gates have been identified, and the funeral chapel of
a Christian martyr, not shown in the plan.

At Histria the wall (fig. 2.2, no. 7), built in the third century
against the Goths, was repeatedly reinforced in the period from Constantine to Justinian, as inscriptions found built into the fabric prove.
In the fifth and sixth centuries, when most of the Western empire
was stagnant, building activity went on vigorously at Histria. Just
inside the main gate (fig. 2.2, no. 4) two basilicas, one secular, one
Christian, were built on the east and south sides of a paved square.
Leading out of the square to the south a paved, drained street was
laid down, parallel to the town wall, flanked by public buildings
(fig. 2.2, no. 5) of basilica type, and by a porticoed market building.
In the southwest corner (fig. 2.2, no. 8) the city wall was extended
to embrace a whole new workers' quarter, with blocks of flimsy
houses, warehouses, a bakery, a butcher's shop, and installations for
the working of artifacts in metal and bone. To the southwest, with a
magnificent view over Lake Sinoe, there rose an "aristocratic" quarter
(fig. 2.2, no. 2), where two houses have been excavated, one with
eight rooms grouped around a peristyle, the other with an apsidal
room (fig. 7.19, right center), which must have been a private chapel,
perhaps for the use of the bishop. The evidence of coins shows that
this late blooming of Histria lasted at least to the reign of Heraclius
(610–41).

Our final example of continuity in Dobruja comes from the huge

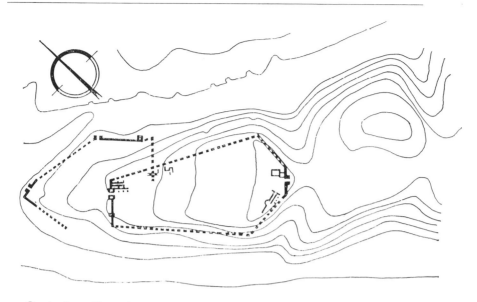

7.18. Axiopolis, plan

7.19. Histria, aristocratic quarter, apsidal room

(eight thousand square meters) necropolis of 811 tombs at Piatra Frecăței (just under Beroe on the map, fig. 2.1), where the burials stretch from the second to the seventh Christian century. Since all the graves are of the inhumation type, the skeletons survive: a significant number of these show the skull deliberately deformed, which we have seen to be a Sarmatian folkway. Since Beroe was a Danube limes fort, we are forced to the conclusion that the Sarmatians, among the barbarians transferred en masse into Dobruja between 340 and 360, served in the Roman army, contributed to the barbarizing of it, and continued to keep their cultural habits intact until the Slavic hordes descended in the seventh century. The Sarmatian presence explains why there is no massive evidence of Slavic predominance in eighth-century Dobruja: the Sarmatians were their kinfolk, and so the Slavs did not overwhelm Dobruja; they were absorbed. One piece of evidence for this is the Romanian language, where the structure is unmistakably Latin: conjugation, declension, numerals, personal pronouns, days of the week, parts of the body, names of relationships. Romanians like to point out that the names of man's part of the farm are Latin: casă, poartă, curte, parete (*parietes,* walls), fereastră (*fenestra,* window); but the animals' part is Slavic: ocol, farmyard; ogradă, paddock; grajd, stable; poiană, clearing. One of the lasting legacies of the long Roman presence in Dobruja is the Latin elegance of the Romanian language.

8. RELIGION,
ARTS, AND CRAFTS

To illustrate religious beliefs, Dacian inscriptions and sculpture have more variety to offer than those of any other Roman province. It is not only the gods of the official state religion that are represented; there is also a whole gamut of divinities from the Greek east and the "barbarian" west: from Asia Minor, Persia, Syria, Egypt, Thrace; from Gaul, Germany, and Mauretania. The explanation of this variety is threefold: first, the influx into the new province, from all over the empire, of merchants bent on exploiting its riches; second, the garrisoning of the many Roman camps with auxiliary troops from other provinces, especially those in the East; third, the tolerance of the Roman administration toward all cults not considered subversive. (Christianity was persecuted because its votaries refused even token worship of the emperors' statues; there is no evidence for Christianity in Dacia until after the Roman withdrawal in 271.) Nor is there unequivocal evidence for the survival of native cults. The main reason for this is that the Dacians did not conceive their gods anthropomorphically: no statues were found in the columned sanctuaries of the Dacian citadels dated in the reigns of Burebista and Decebalus. But there is little doubt that behind the ostensible dedications to some Greco-Roman gods—for example, six to Liber, god of wine at Drobeta; and others elsewhere to Diana the Huntress, Silvanus, god of the forest, Hercules the Strong Man—lie native divinities identified with the classical pantheon by the process known to historians of religion as syncretism, or *interpretatio Romana.*

All the gods of the Roman pantheon are represented in Dacia. They are most memorably recorded in the two lines of hexameter verse into which, with considerable virtuosity, the Roman epic poet Ennius compressed them:

> Iuno, Vesta, Minerva, Ceres, Diana, Venus, Mars,
> Mercurius, Iovis, Neptunus, Vulcanus, Apollo.

From the *embarras de richesses,* epigraphical and artistic, which might be used for illustration, I select two, both from Cioroiul Nou (ancient Aquae, some forty miles west of Romula; see map, fig. 5.1). Figure 8.1 shows a marble head of Apollo, crowned with laurel, and originally painted in polychrome; figure 8.2 represents Liber-Bacchus, the one god omitted from Ennius's canon, possibly because at the time the lines were written the cult was in bad odor. The Dacian marble head shows the god crowned with grape clusters, his hair showing traces of brick-red paint.

Twenty percent of the inscriptions found in Dacia refer to Oriental cults, whose popularity begins in the mid-second century of our era. They express the nostalgia of their votaries, serving Rome or Mammon far from home; they were popular because they were less austere than the official religion and because they promised salvation and immortality. From Asia Minor came Cybele, the Phrygian Earth Mother, and her votary Attis, who emasculated himself for her sake; Mēn, the moon god; Glycon, the Paphlagonian tutelary divinity, worshiped in the form of a snake; and the Phrygian Sabazius, equated with Liber-Bacchus, and receiving from his worshipers offerings of votive bronze hands, adorned with a bewildering variety of cult symbols: pine-cone, eagle, ram's head, tortoise, snake, caduceus (snake-wreathed wand), winnowing fan, frog, basket, lizard.[1] From Persia came Mithras, god of light, most popular among soldiers; over 274 dedications to him are known in Dacia. Figure 8.3 shows a typical Mithraic scene, carved probably in the Severan period. It comes from Ulpia Traiana, and is in the Deva museum. The god, in a Phrygian cap and with his cloak streaming in the wind, is slaying the bull in whose blood his worshipers will be washed, guaranteeing them immortality. Animals accompany him: a dog, a snake, a scorpion, a lion. To the left is Cautopates, with reversed torch, symbolizing the sunset of death; to the right Cautes, symbolizing the sunrise of eternal life. At the left edge is Mithras carrying the slain bull; at the right, a person in Eastern dress; behind him, the

1. Compare the hand from Avenches, Switzerland, in MacKendrick, *Romans on the Rhine,* fig. 6.14.

8.1. Cioroiul Nou, Apollo   8.2. Cioroiul Nou, Bacchus

8.3. Ulpia Traiana, Mithras

cliff from which Mithras was born. The figures were intended to be seen silhouetted against a light shining from behind.

From Syria came Atargatis and Astarte, both equated with Venus, and Jupiter with various cult titles, e.g., Dolichenus, from Doliche in the east Anatolian puppet state of Commagene. A fragment of a bronze plaque from Răcari, forty miles east of Drobeta, shows him armed with cuirass, sword, and double ax, and standing on a bull.

From Egypt came Serapis and Isis, of which more will be said below in connection with sculptured heads from Tomis. Isis-worship in Dacia is attested on four inscriptions from Ulpia Traiana, three from Apulum, two from Micia, and one each from Romula and Potaissa; the last-mentioned implies the existence of a temple. But the most interesting evidence for Isis-cult in Dacia is the head of a smiling baby boy (fig. 8.4) from Drobeta, now in the Bucharest museum. Though his hair is close-cropped in front, he wears it in two long locks at the back, unfortunately not visible in the photograph. This coiffure was worn by children whose parents had dedicated them to the service of the goddess.

From Thrace and Moesia came the cults of Bendis, equated with Artemis, and the Thracian Rider. A bronze appliqué of the first century B.C., found in the Dacian citadel of Piatra Roșie, represents Bendis (fig. 8.5). The eyes, now empty, were rendered in glass paste. She wears a turban on her head; perhaps she held a pine bough in her upraised hands. A lead plaque from Romula (fig. 8.6) represents a pair of Thracian or Danubian riders, heraldically facing the Great Mother, who wears a coronet, sits cross-legged, and holds their horses by the bridles. Over their heads floats the Dacian dragon-standard, familiar from Trajan's Column. Beneath their horses' feet they trample an enemy, symbol of the triumph of good over evil. In the upper register are crude representations of the sun god, men with fish; of victories, an eagle; and of the moon goddess. In the lower register are seen a bull, a lion, a candelabrum, wreaths, and tripods.

The most important Celtic cult attested in Dacia is that of the horse-goddess Epona; among Germanic goddesses, the fertility deities called Matronae deserve mention.[2] Their worshipers were either Celts

2. They are illustrated, from their home ground, in ibid., figs. 6.8 and 6.9.

8.4. Drobeta, child

8.5. Piatra Roșie, Bendis

8.6. Romula, Danubian Rider, lead plaque

and Germans stationed in Dacia or Dacians returned from long tours of duty in the West. The *di patrii* of the Moors, mentioned on a temple inscription of the Severan age from Micia, will remind us of Lusius Quietus's Moorish cavalry, figured on Trajan's Column.

Finally, a piece of evidence for Christianity in Dacia: a pierced bronze inscription of the fourth century from Biertan, in southern Transylvania (fig. 5.1), now in Bucharest. It records (fig. 8.7) that one Zenovius made the offering. The pendant bears, in a circle, the chi-rho monogram, the first two letters of Christ's name in Greek, but the inscription is in Latin, a testimony to the survival of Roman culture in Dacia after Aurelian's withdrawal.

In Dobruja, Greek cults are naturally more prevalent, given the long Greek associations of the coastal cities, which for over a millennium remained extraordinarily faithful to the gods of the motherland, including, at Tomis alone, Dionysus, Apollo, Aphrodite, Asclepius, the Dioscuri (Castor and Pollux), the Eleusinian triad (Demeter, Pluto, Persephone), and Poseidon. But the official cult of Rome and the emperor is not absent, nor are Mēn, Mithras, the Thracian Rider, Fortuna, Nemesis, Glycon, Isis, or Sarapis.[3] We have already noted the evidence for Christianity, in the numerous fifth-century basilicas found at Tropaeum Traiani, Troesmis, and the coastal cities.

A curious piece of evidence for the worship of the Phrygian god Mēn, perhaps the counterpart of Attis, is provided by a huge sarcophagus of the first or second century in the courtyard of the Museum of Archaeology in Constanţa (fig. 8.8). Its symbols, never satisfactorily explained, include a whip, a bell, a pair of scales, a bull's head, a double ax, and a spear.

A cave at Gura Dobrogei, eighteen miles north of Constanţa, yielded a first- or second-century relief of Mithras slaying the bull, with the same symbols as on the piece from Ulpia Traiana described above. Since two altars and a marble tabletop were also found in the cave, it is clear that it was an actual place of Mithraic worship, the shrines of the god being regularly underground.

The Thracian Rider is represented on a remarkably primitive relief of the second or third century, from Tomis (fig. 8.9). The propor-

---

3. The god is usually spelled Serapis in Latin, Sarapis in Greek.

8.7. Biertan, Christian
à jour ornament

8.8. Constanța,
Mēn sarcophagus

8.9. Tomis,
Thracian Rider,
relief

tions are all wrong: for example, the rider's head is bigger than the horse's; but the dog and the boar beneath have a certain quaint charm.

The twenty-four pieces of sculpture found together in Constanţa in 1962 (fig. 6.7) are more in the conventional Greek tradition. They date from the Severan age. Three are of particular interest. The first (fig. 8.10) is the majestic standing figure of a goddess wearing a diadem and carrying a horn of plenty. She is the Fortuna or Tychê —Lady Luck—of the city. The miniature, bushy-bearded, naked figure at her feet symbolizes the Black Sea. He wears a turreted crown, is leaning on a ship, and carries a rudder. The second piece worthy of remark is an aedicula, or miniature temple, containing twin figures of Nemesis, goddess of vengeance. They carry in their hands rods calibrated like yardsticks, with which they measure the just and unjust actions of mankind. The detail of one of the heads (fig. 8.11) shows a great sensitivity of execution. The third piece is the most famous. Out of a single block of marble is carved—a tour de force—a snake in eight coils. His upraised head has human ears and hair, but the muzzle of a ruminant—goat or camel (fig. 8.12). Interpretations vary: it may be the snake of the healing god Asclepius, or a Hellenistic good-luck *daimon* called Glycon.

Egyptian worship is represented by heads of Isis and Sarapis. The Isis (fig. 8.13) is Flavian work, in the tradition of the great Praxiteles, much finer in execution than the priestess in figure 6.5. She wears the crescent moon in her hair and has two small horns; her locks fall in corkscrew ringlets to her shoulders. The Sarapis is Antonine, conceived as a tragic figure. Sarapis is remarkable as the only pagan god created by a committee. Ptolemy I of Egypt (reigned 307/306–283/282) decreed his existence in order to unify the Greeks and the Egyptians in his kingdom: Sarapis combined the attributes of a number of Greek gods with some of the characteristics of Osiris, god of the Egyptian underworld, and incarnation of the deceased Pharaoh. In Egypt and in Dacia and Moesia, his worshipers tended to be men of high rank, prefects, legates, and centurions. On the committee to create him were Manetho, an Egyptian priest who wrote a history of his country in Greek, and two Athenians: Demetrius of Phalerum, philosopher, tyrant, and librarian; and Timotheus, an aristocrat who was hierophant (high priest) of the Eleusinian Mysteries.

8.10. Tomis, Fortuna

8.11. Tomis, Nemesis, detail

8.12. Tomis, Glycon

8.13. Tomis, Isis, Flavian

So much for art in the service of religion. Thus far in this book we have used art in ancient Romania largely as documentation. It is now time to inquire, with the emphasis on sculpture, whether this is all it deserves. It should be clear by now that in Moesia and Dacia, in the sphere of the arts, the Romans were not bringing the blessings of civilization to an undeveloped country. In Moesia, the artistic tradition went back to Neolithic times: witness the Cernavoda Thinker (fig. 1.2). Histria had been in the mainstream of the archaic and classical Greek tradition in architecture, ceramics, and glyptics (figs. 2.8, 10–12). Callatis flourished artistically in the fourth century B.C. and in Hellenistic times (figs. 2.17, 18, and 20). In Dacia we have seen (figs. 3.6–10, 13–17) how sophisticated architecture was in the reigns of Burebista and Decebalus; the DECEBAL PER SCORILO vase (fig. 3.18) shows a certain competence in Dacian potters; the Bendis from Piatra Roşie (fig. 8.5) hints at what Dacian sculpture might have become if Rome had not intervened. But Rome did intervene and we must ask ourselves what difference the intervention made in the art of her Romanian provinces. The evidence I offer comes mainly from Dobruja. Art flourished there because of the long Greek tradition and because of the prosperity attendant upon the *pax Romana*.

The Romans regarded art as functional, in two areas, official and personal. We have seen enough examples of Roman official, propagandistic art: on Trajan's Column (figs. 4.3–13, 15–20), in the wolf and twins of Apulum (fig. 5.9) and Ibida (fig. 6.4), in the Caracalla of Porolissum (fig. 5.12), and the Decius of Ulpia Traiana (fig. 5.13). I show one more propaganda piece, rare if not unique in Trajanic iconography: a marble head, probably from Callatis, in the Severeanu collection in Bucharest, showing Trajan, face lined and drawn, cheeks sunken, in the last stages of the wasting disease that killed him in 117 (fig. 8.14). It has the stark realism of the "death-mask" sculpture of the Roman republic; it is a pious and moving tribute to the "best of princes" in the last year of his life.

But in the examples about to be presented, which were not chosen to fit a thesis, it is the other area of Roman functional art that is represented: the use of art to adorn personal life, without official prescription, and to honor one's gods and one's family, alive and dead. This the expression of the personal side of that sense of loyalty

that the Romans called *pietas*. The gods, first. Besides the examples
adduced in figures 8.1–13, I add two more of special interest artistically. The first is a marble head of Aphrodite from Tomis (fig.
8.15). It is earlier than the rest (first or second century of our era),
and, even in its mutilated state, reveals a softness and serenity that is
a living heritage from the Hellenistic age. It is characteristic classicizing of the philhellene Hadrian's time, not Roman but Greek, and
not derivative but obviously part of a living Hellenic tradition. My
second example comes from Ulpia Traiana and is dated in the second
century. It is a charming bronze statuette, less than twenty inches
high, of a child (fig. 8.16) who has not yet lost his baby fat. The
pudgy quality and the parody of the Praxitelean S-curve stance are
infinitely appealing, the work of a master. The boy bears a resemblance to the chubby, effeminate Attis from Trier, as yet un-
castrated.[4]

4. See MacKendrick, *Romans on the Rhine,* fig. 6.15.

8.14. Callatis, Trajan   8.15. Tomis, Aphrodite

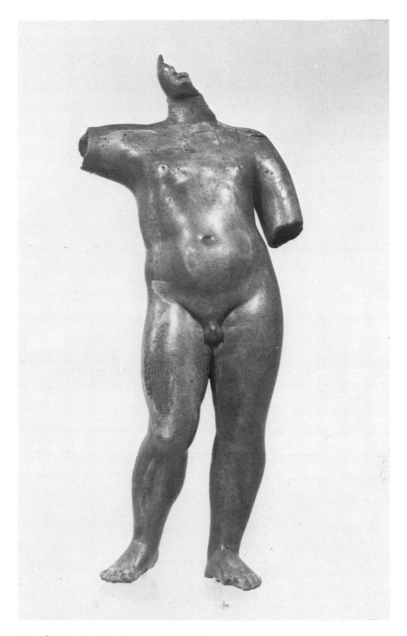

8.16. Ulpia Traiana, child, bronze

I illustrate more personal expressions of pietas with three examples. The first is in the Constanța museum, the marble head (second century) of a handsome sleeping young man (fig. 8.17), from Ostrov, previously mentioned as the necropolis of the Roman camp at Durostorum. It represents—and sentimentalizes—Death, after the rather saccharine manner of Hadrianic classicizing, but, like the Tomis Aphrodite, it shows that the Greek tradition and Greek technical skill are not yet dead. The second example of the use of art for the adornment of personal life is the idealized head of a girl from Tomis (fig. 8.18). Since she wears her hair in the style of Faustina the Elder, consort of Marcus Aurelius, she is dated 160–70. The upturned eyes and downturned mouth give the face a resigned and pathetic expression, appropriate to a grave monument. The head classicizes sentimentality again, a generation later than Hadrian, and this time more Roman than Greek. Third, the marble head of an ephebe (adolescent boy), early third century, from Tropaeum Traiani (fig. 8.19). This is the kind of statue that in the Greek world was set up in a gymnasium to honor a good-looking young athlete. It is interesting to see this Greek custom being followed, in a Hellenistic sculptural style, in a Roman city like Tropaeum Traiani.

So far, the examples shown have all been technically competent. The other side of the story is the impact of Greco Roman sculptural tradition on native stonecutters, where the result is folk art. We have seen this already, on the propaganda side, in the metopes of Adamclisi (figs. 4.21–30). On the personal side, I offer two examples. The first (fig. 8.20) is a marble relief (second to third century) from Tomis, trying its best to represent the three Graces. A less graceful trio would be hard to imagine, with their long torsos, stumpy legs, and the contorsionist effect produced by the head of the central figure. This is a valiant attempt to render, probably from a pattern book, familiar figures from Greek mythology, by a stonecutter who is not so much incompetent as not—to use Matthew Arnold's word—"penetrated" by the slightest concept of what Greek art was trying to do. Such refinement was simply not part of his experience. The attempt to make it so is part of the snobbish hypocrisy attendant upon the acceptance of an alien art by a native population; it is what gives the word "provincial" a bad name. What native artists could do when they knew and liked what they were doing is illustrated by the Piatra Roşie Bendis (fig. 8.5).

8.17. Ostrov, Death

8.18. Tomis, idealized girl

8.19. Tropaeum Traiani, ephebe,
marble head

8.20. Tomis, the three Graces, relief

8.21. Căşei, grave stele

8.22. Sucidava,
"Moor," terra-cotta

The second example is a third-century sandstone grave relief from
Căşei, in Transylvania (fig. 8.21), now in the Bucharest Museum of
National History. The deceased, identified in the inscription as an
army veteran, is portrayed wrapped in a sheepskin, reclining as he
partakes of a banquet. He hands a festive garland to his wife, who
is sitting in a chair. Before them is a three-legged table, its top
turned down to show the silver service. Above them, three servants
hold up lengths of pleated cloth; perhaps our veteran had gone into
business as a draper. In the upper register, a pair of peacocks feed
on grapes; they are flanked by *genii,* the ancestors of the Christian
guardian angels. Beside the *genius* on the left is dimly seen a bull's
head. This is folk art of an honester sort. The veteran knew, and
told the stonecutter, exactly what he wanted: it was his bad luck—
and our good fortune, for it is an entertaining piece—that good
sculptors were rare in third-century Căşei.

Finally, a word about the archaeological evidence for crafts in Roman
Dacia and Moesia. It must be brief, for the evidence is much sparser
that that, for example, from Roman Gaul.[5] Both literary and archaeological sources agree that farming was the chief occupation of
Dacia and Moesia; in Roman times they were two of the principal
granaries of the empire, as we know from the testimony of numerous
finds of farm tools, and from the villas, both rustic and suburban.
Viticulture was an important branch of farming; a relief of 150–200
from Făgăraşul Nou, near Hîrşova in Dobruja, shows two men
treading grapes in a vat; beside them waits a two-wheeled oxcart
laden with a huge barrel. Cattle-raising, with its subsidiaries, tanning
and shoemaking, was also important. A terra-cotta head of a Negro
or Moor, of the early third century (fig. 8.22), found at Sucidava,
may portray an agricultural laborer, though we must remember that
most slaves in antiquity were not black. And his crown of vine leaves
and his necklace with a crescent moon put his slave status in doubt.

   5. See MacKendrick, *Roman France.* figs. 7.1-16.

Let us recall that what attracted the Romans to Dacia in the first place was its mineral wealth, especially its gold: it had the richest mines in Europe. We saw that the mines, once the monopoly of the Dacian kings, became a monopoly of the Roman emperors, who administered them, under lease, through a vast bureaucracy of overseers, sub-overseers, registrars, bookkeepers, paymasters, and file-clerks. Expert miners were imported from Dalmatia. The ordinary mine workers were poor freemen, often illiterate, or slaves, who were branded and chained, and subject to lashing by a military guard. We know most about the mines from a series of twenty-five wax tablets, found in the last century. They range in date from 131 to 167, and were hidden in the mine tunnels during the panic of Marcus Aurelius's Marcomannic wars. Their subjects are various: contracts of purchase and sale, mine-rental, receipts for loans repaid, the details of the dissolution of a burial society. From them we learn that a six-year-old girl sold for 205 denarii—the price of forty-one pigs or fifty-seven sheep. The narrowness of the mine tunnels suggests that she was one of the unfortunates used for child labor. A Greek boy sold for 600 denarii, a Greek woman for 420. One tablet records the menu of a burial-society dinner: one lamb, one piglet, white bread, two kinds of wine (over fifty times as much *ordinaire* as good wine was consumed), vinegar, salt, onions, and incense for the sacrifice. The tablet illustrated (figs. 8.23a and 8.23b) comes from Alburnus Maior (Roşia Montană), is dated June 20, 162, and records a loan made by a Roman to a native woman at 1 percent per month on the unpaid balance. Over one hundred inscriptions refer to the mines; though the wax tablets stop in 167, the inscriptions continue, and show that the mines were still worked though with reduced production; perhaps the veins were giving out. In the mine tunnels were found tools, pit-props, and a waterwheel for keeping the mine dry.

Other minerals found in Dacia were silver, copper, iron, and lead. The country was also rich in building-stone: marble, limestone, andesite, sandstone, and schist. Salt was another valuable commodity. From Valea Florilor, in idyllic country fifteen miles south of Apahida, full of carved and painted wooden farmhouses and smiling green fields, was reported in 1971 a deposit of wooden extracting tools, preserved by the salt in which they were found. The tools found were shovels, paddles, pokers, levers, hooks, tampers, and a

8.23a. Alburnus Maior, wax tablet

8.23b. Alburnus Maior, wax tablet, continuation

20-by-77-inch lindenwood trough with pegged holes in the bottom, which must have been used as a settling basin.

The potter's was a major craft: he made native wares, imitations of Italian or Gaulish terra sigillata, lamps, and tiles. One of the most charming products of a Dacian kiln is the child's toy horse and cart (fig. 8.24) found in Transylvania, and now in the Bucharest museum. Related to the potter's craft was that of cameo-making (especially at Romula) and glass-blowing (especially at Tomis).

A gravestone from Tomis shows the importance of seafaring there; besides a Thracian Rider approaching a priest at an altar, it portrays a merchant ship with square sail and crew (fig. 8.25).

Finally, also from Tomis, an early third-century limestone grave-stele portrays a follower of the most bloodthirsty of occupations, the long-haired Dacian gladiator Skirtos (fig. 8.26). He is dressed in skins and holds in his left hand a long trident and a dagger. His right hand holds a shorter trident at which his pet dog looks up. The inscription states that he won six victories, but died before his time.

8.24. Transylvania, toy horse and cart, terra-cotta

8.25. Tomis, grave stele with merchant ship

8.26. Tomis, grave stele of gladiator

On this characteristically homely, bloodthirsty, and tragic note we end our archaeological history of ancient Romania. A tragic note, because one of the sober lessons of archaeology is that man is born to trouble as the sparks fly upward. In Romania, the elegant Neolithic culture is overthrown by the crude invaders who brought the Bronze Age. Histria, in touch with the main movement of the Greek mind in the archaic and classical periods, declines with the silting of its harbor, suffers sack by Dacians and Goths, ekes out an existence by time-serving under the Romans, and finally succumbs, after thirteen hundred years, to the hordes of the Slavs and the Avars. Burebista unites his people and is assassinated; Decebalus stands heroically against the Romans and is driven to suicide. The Romans, after 165 years of imperialist effort, cut their losses and retire from Dacia. Dobruja lasts longer as a Roman province, but is racked by wave after wave of barbarian invasion. The late empire retrenches in Dobruja, but the whole province finally succumbs to the same barbarians who leveled Histria to the ground. In religion, native and classical cults yield to the alien salvation-religions from the East, including Christianity. In architecture, the Romans level to the ground the splendid Dacian citadels. In sculpture, the Greek tradition in Dobruja struggles to survive, but sculptors imitate and become less and less creative; craftsmen become less and less competent, and a thousand-year-old tradition ends not with a bang but a whimper.

But this is only the dark side of the picture. Archaeology has another lesson to teach: it speaks of the essential indestructibility of man in his striving for beauty and for freedom. Neolithic man in Romania created the beauty of the Cernavoda Thinker and the Cucuteni pots; at Hăbășești village we have an early and heartening example of man's capacity as a social animal. The Greek colonies of Dobruja kept the glorious tradition of the motherland alive, in the arts, religion, and politics, for well over a thousand years. In Dacia, Burebista and Decebalus created a culture that it would be narrow-minded to call "barbarian," and the heroism of Decebalus and his people against overwhelming odds evoked the admiration of their conquerors. The Romans in Dacia were more than mere gold-grubbers: they brought the culture of sophisticated cities, the rule of law, the Roman peace. In Dobruja, their tolerance kept Greek culture alive for five generations after their empire had crumbled in the West. In religion, the Christian basilica borrows the majesty of great Roman secular buildings: the pope in Rome is a legitimate descendant of Western emperors, the patriarch in Constantinople of Byzantine kings. In art, the remarkable thing is not the decadence but the survival of the classical heritage: Justinian's Santa Sophia in Constantinople would have been impossible without Hadrian's Pantheon in Rome. In 421, in the Byzantine capital, Theodosius II finished the column whose sculptured scroll recorded the victory of his grandfather, Theodosius I, over the Goths; it was Trajan's Column over again. Dobrujan potters and jewelers kept their crafts alive and taught them to their Slavic conquerors.

"Slavic conquerors" is a misnomer. The Slavs never conquered the Romanians: they were absorbed by them. The proof is the Romanian language, a Latin island in a Slavic sea. That Romania today is Greek Orthodox in religion and Western in its cultural orientation is due to its Greco-Roman heritage that archaeology has described in this book. When a modern Romanian wishes you bon voyage, he says, "Drum bun." The "drum" is Greek, the "bun" is Latin. It is no small tribute to the staying power of the Roman Empire that when the Dacian stones speak, their language is Greek and Latin.

CHRONOLOGY
CHAPTER BIBLIOGRAPHIES
INDEX

CHRONOLOGY

Neolithic and Bronze Age dates are controversial and only approximate. I follow those given in excavation reports or accepted by the authorities of the Museum of National History.

B.C.

3000	Cernavoda, Neolithic sculpture
3000–2700	Izvoare
2700–2000	Cucuteni, Neolithic pottery
2700–1800	Hăbăşeşti village
2600–2400	Troy I
2000	Late Neolithic: Pietrele fox
2000–1800	Cucuteni B destroyed

1800–1200 Bronze Age

1800–1500	Perşinari, gold treasure
1700–1300	Monteoru culture
1300	Wietenberg culture
1250–1125	Transition to Iron Age: Uioara de Sus

1200–500 Iron Age I (Hallstatt): Ferigile

900–800	Rafaila
700–500	Poiana (Piroboridava)
657 or 625	Histria founded
6th–5th century	Tomis and Callatis founded; Histria, temple of Zeus Polieus
560	Megara founds Heraclea Pontica
512	Scythian expedition of Darius of Persia

500–1 B.C. Iron Age II (La Tène)

5th–4th century	Zimnicea, Getic settlement
ca. 450	Histria, democratic regime imposed

4th century	Agighiol silver treasure; Cotofănești gold helmet; Callatis wall and papyrus grave
367/366–283/282	Ptolemy I, king of Egypt
364/363–353/352	Clearchus, tyrant of Heraclea Pontica
348	Philip II of Macedon against Thracians
339	Philip II against Scythians
335	Alexander crosses Danube
313	Histria revolts against Lysimachus of Thrace
310/309	Lysimachus besieges Callatis
late 4th century	Histria, sacred area burnt; Callatis, ustrinum
4th–2d century	Histria, Hellenistic wall; Callatis, gilt terra-cotta miniatures
3d century	Poroina rhyton; Histria, temple of Aphrodite; Piscul Crăsanilor, Dacian settlement; Celts in Transylvania
292	Lysimachus prisoner, perhaps in Piscul Crăsanilor
281	Death of Lysimachus
279	Celts attack Histria and Delphi
262	Histria and Callatis war against Byzantium
251	Theoros from Callatis
230–130	Ciumești necropolis
200	Callatis building inscription
200–150	Histria ephebe inscription
2d century (?)	Histria aqueduct
2d–1st century	Popești flourishes
145–72	Tilișca counterfeiter's coins
110–72/71	Mithridates controls Pontic cities
early 80s	Burebista moves capital from Popești to Costești
80s B.C.–A.D. 106	Dacian citadels
72/71	Callatis treaty with Rome
61	Coalition of Greeks and barbarians defeats C. Antonius Hybrida at Histria
after 50	Histria, "second founding"
44	Burebista assassinated
42	Geto-Dacian contingent with Brutus at Philippi

27 B.C.–A.D. 14 Augustus

27	Crassus triumphs over Geto-Dacians
14 B.C.–A.D. 98	Minor Dacian citadels flourish

A.D.

6–12	Sex. Aelius Catus destroys Muntenian towns
9–17	Ovid in exile at Tomis
12	Barbarians attack Aegyssus

14–37 Tiberius

14	Barbarians attack Troesmis; Dobruja becomes province of Moesia
15–35	C. Poppaeus Sabinus, governor of Moesia
26	Poppaeus crushes Dobrujan revolt

41–54 Claudius

ca. 49	Histria's fishing rights guaranteed

54–68 Nero: Noviodunum camp founded

57–67	Ti. Plautius Silvanus Aelianus, governor of Moesia
60–65	Columella, agricultural writer, flourishes

81–96 Domitian: Bărboși naval base founded

85–89	Dacian War; Hadrian commands Legio V Macedonica
86	Moesia divided into two provinces
87–106	Decebalus, king of Dacia
87	Cornelius Fuscus defeated and killed at Tapae
88	Tettius Julianus defeats Decebalus at Tapae
92	Angustia diploma

98–117 Trajan

101–2	First Dacian War: camps at Drobeta, Sucidava, Romula, Dierna, Tibiscum, Bucium (Orăştioara), Arcidava, Centum Putei, Berzobis, Micia, Gilău, Bologa (?), Buciumi, Tihău-Odorhei line, Mălăeşti, Drajna de Sus, Angustia (?), Bumbeşti, Răcari
105	Drobeta, stone camp
105–6	Second Dacian War: Limes Alutanus: Buridava, Slăveni, Arutela; camps at Potaissa, Napoca, Porolissum; Ulmetum; Danube limes; Apulum municipium
108–10	Ulpia Traiana founded
109	Tropaeum Traiani, trophy and town
112	Legio V Macedonica at Troesmis
113	Trajan's Column dedicated in Rome

117–38 Hadrian: Mălăeşti, Drajna de Sus, Tîrgşor abandoned; Rădăcineşti camp built; Răcari rebuilt in stone

118	Hadrian visits Dobruja; Apulum becomes seat of government of Dacia
124	Dacia divided into three provinces; Hadrian visits Dobruja and Napoca; Napoca and Drobeta become municipia
131–67	Alburnus Maior gold mines flourish
132	Ulpia Traiana amphitheater built
133	Gherla diploma

138–61 Antoninus Pius: Moors garrison Răcari; Dobruja flourishes; Capidava, a customs-station

138–222	Hobiţa villa rustica flourishes
143	Căşei camp
148	Gilău camp rebuilt
before 150	Orheiul Bistriţei, military tile kiln
157	Arcidava, Micia, stone camps; Porolissum amphitheater rebuilt in stone

| 158 | Ulpia Traiana amphitheater repaired |
| 160 | Costoboci invade |

161–80 Marcus Aurelius

160–70	Tomis, idealized head of girl
162–72, 177–80	Marcomannic War: Ulpia Traiana suburban villas burned; Slăveni camp destroyed; Citera camp at Porolissum rebuilt in stone
167/68	Legio V Macedonica transferred from Troesmis to Potaissa; Apulum military headquarters for all Dacia

180–93 Commodus: Napoca colony; no-man's-land on northwest frontier

| 180–83 | Sucidava customs-station |

193–211 Septimius Severus: Limes Transalutanus built: fourteen camps Flăminda-Cumidava, including Jidava; Apahida villa rustica; Romula: brick circuit-wall, curia

193–98	Drobeta, Romula, Apulum, Porolissum, Dierna, Ampelum made colonies
195	Potaissa baths enlarged
201	Bumbeşti camp rebuilt in stone
202	Severus in Dobruja
204	Micia, Moors' temple
205	Slăveni camp rebuilt

211–17 Caracalla: Mănerau villa rustica; Potaissa colony; Bologa and Buciumi rebuilt

212	Decree of universal citizenship
213	Caracalla visits Porolissum
215	Last evidence of Roman gold-mining

217 Macrinus: honored by Histria

217–22 Elagabalus: Bucium (Orăştioara) camp walls repaired

222–35 Severus Alexander: Council of Three Dacias meets at Ulpia
Traiana; Ad Mediam camp restored; Micia
amphitheater goes out of use

229   Dio Cassius consul
230–40   Arutela, last coins

235–38 Maximinus Thrax: road repairs in Dobruja

238–44 Gordian III: Potaissa basilica; Carpi invade Dobruja

244–49 Philip the Arab: Carpi raid Răcari, Jidava: Limes Transalutanus abandoned; Sucidava, stone circuit-
wall; Bumbeşti, last coins

247   Millennium of Rome celebrated
248   Romula, circuit wall, third phase; Goths invade
                             Moesia

249–51 Decius

251   Porolissum (Pomet) camp repaired; Decius dies
                             in battle

260–68 Gallienus: Ulpia Traiana, Porolissum, latest coins; Goths
sack Tibiscum; usurper Regalianus claims de-
scent from Decebalus

263   Sarmatians burn Callatis extramural quarter
267   Histria sacked; wall rebuilt

268–70 Claudius Gothicus: Goths attack Tomis; Claudius beats them
at Naissus

270–75 Aurelian

271   Dacia officially abandoned

275–76 Tacitus: detachment of Legio XIII Gemina at Desa (to 305)

284–305 Diocletian: Dinogetia citadel; Capidava rebuilt

295	Goths destroy Tropaeum Traiani
3d-4th century	Tîrgşor, Sarmatian necropolis

306–37 Constantine I: Drobeta, Ulmetum, Axiopolis camps rebuilt; Tomis, mosaic building

316	Tropaeum Traiani rebuilt
317	Constantine's son Crispus appointed Caesar
324–30	Constantinople built

324–61 Constantius II: Tomis renamed for him (?)

328	Romula milestone; Sucidava and Constantiniana Daphne bridges
337	Capidava rebuilt
340–60	Barbarians transferred en masse into Dobruja

364–75 Valentinian I: coins at Porolissum

375	Huns sack Dinogetia

364–78 Valens

367	Constantiniana Daphne and Noviodunum bridges; Pietroasa treasure

379–95 Theodosius I: coins at Apulum, Porolissum

4th century	Biertan Christian inscription

383–408 Arcadius: coins at Dierna

408–50 Theodosius II: coins at Napoca; gold treasure of Someşeni

421	Column of Theodosius II, Constantinople
441–43	Attila and Huns sack Răcari, Drobeta
447	Attila and Huns sack Sucidava
ca. 450	Huns sack Ulpia Traiana: amphitheater used as fort
late 5th century	Huns sack Capidava, Ulmetum

491–518 Anastasius I: rebuilds Dinogetia; Callatis, "Syrian" basilica

527–65 Justinian: coins at Dierna, Micia; rebuilding of Drobeta,
Sucidava, Capidava, Ulmetum, Axiopolis,
Troesmis east citadel; Tomis and Histria walls;
Tropaeum Traiani, "marble" basilica, Phase
III; Histria, internal bath buildings

559   Dinogetia falls

582–602 Maurice: rebuilds Ulmetum

after 586   Avars and Slavs destroy Tropaeum Traiani
596/97   Avars and Slavs sack Sucidava, Dinogetia,
Capidava, Ulmetum

610–41 Heraclius: Histria survives; Piatra Frecăţei necropolis

704   Tomis falls to Slavs

CHAPTER
BIBLIOGRAPHIES

Research in Romanian archaeology requires a reading knowledge of Romanian, which, fortunately, can be acquired in six weeks by anyone conversant with Latin or another Romance language. However, in the bibliography that follows, where there is a choice between a source in Romanian and one in one of the scholarly languages of western Europe, I have chosen the latter. With characteristic courtesy, the Romanians keep the world archaeologically up to date in their journal *Dacia*, with articles exclusively in the Western languages; and most articles in Romanian are published with résumés in French, German, or Italian—less often in English.

I. ROMANIA IN PREHISTORY

Berciu, Dumitru. *Necropole de incinerație din epoca bronzului de la Cîrna*. Bucharest, 1961.
———. *Romania. Ancient Peoples and Places*. London, 1967.
Dumitrescu, Vladimir. *L'art néolithique en Roumanie*. Bucharest, 1968.
———. *Muzeul Național de Antichități*. Bucharest, 1968.
    Convenient brief catalogue of the classical collection of the Museum of National History.
Dumitrescu, Vladimir, and Dumitrescu, Hortensia. *Hăbășești*. Monumentele Patriei Noastre. Bucharest, 1967.
Florescu, Marilene. "Etapile timpurii de culturii Monteoru în Moldova." *Arheologia Moldovei* 4 (1966): 38–118.
Florescu, Radu. *Ghid arheologic al Dobrogei*. Bucharest, 1968.
    Very useful.
Gimbutas, Marija. *Bronze Age Cultures of Central and Eastern Europe*. The Hague, 1965.
Horedt, Kurt. "Așezările fortificate din prima vîrsta a fierului în Transilvania." *Probleme de muzeografie* 5 (1960): 179–87.
Iliescu, Octavian. "Tezaurul de obiecte premonetare de aur din epoca bronzului, găsit la Perșinari (Tîrgoviște)." *Caiet selectiv de informare asupra creșterii colecțiilor bibliotecei Academiei R. P. R.* 8 (1962): 414–18.

Petrescu-Dîmbovița, Mircea. *Cucuteni*. Monumentele Patriei Noastre. Bucharest, 1966.

Schmidt, Hubert. *Cucuteni in der oberen Moldau*. Berlin-Leipzig, 1932. Exemplary; fine color plates.

Stoian, Iorgu. *Tomitana*. Biblioteca de Arheologie, vol. 6. Bucharest, 1962.

Volpe, Alexandru. *Ferigile*. Bucharest, 1967.

Vulpe, Radu, and Vulpe, Ecaterina. "La Civilisation dace et ses problèmes à la lumière des dernières fouilles de Poiana en Basse-Moldavie." *Dacia* 3–4 (1927–32): 253–351.

———. *Izvoare*. Biblioteca de Arheologie, vol. 1. Bucharest, 1957.

2. GREEK COLONIES ON THE BLACK SEA

Alexandrescu, Petre, and Eftimie, Victoria. "Tombes thraces d'époque archaïque dans la nécropole tumulaire d'Histria." *Dacia,* n.s. 3 (1959): 143–64.

Berciu, Dumitru. *Arte traco-getice*. Biblioteca de Arheologie, vol. 14. Bucharest, 1969.

———. "O descoperire traco-scitică din Dobrogea și problema scitică la Dunărea de Jos." *Studii și cercetări de istorie veche* 10 (1959): 7–48.

———. "Descoperirile getice de la Cernavoda (1954) și unele aspecte ale începutului formării culturii La Tène geto-dacic la Dunărea de Jos." *Materiale și cercetări arheologice* 4 (1957): 281–317.

———. "Das thrako-getische Fürstengrab von Agighiol in Rumänien." *Bericht der Römisch-Germanischen Kommission des Deutschen Archäologischen Instituts* 50 (1969): 239–65.

Bordenache, Gabriella. *Sculture greche e romane nel Museo Nazionale di Antichità*. Bucharest, 1969.

Bucovală, Mihai. *Necropole elenistice la Tomis*. Constanța, 1966.

Canarache, Vasile. *Masks and Tanagra Figurines, Made in the Workshops of Callatis-Mangalia*. Constanța, 1969.

———. *Tomis*. Monumentele Patriei Noastre. Bucharest, 1961.

Condurachi, Emil. In *Istoria Romîniei,* edited by Constantin Daicoviciu et al, vol. 1, pp. 162–76.

———. *Histria*. 2d ed. Monumentele Patriei Noastre. Bucharest, 1968.

———. "Influences grecques et romaines dans les Balkans." In *Le rayonnement des civilisations grecques et romaines sur les cultures péripheriques*. Paris, 1965.

———. "Santierul arheologic Histria." *Materiale și cercetări arheologice* 9 (1970): 177–225.

————, ed. *Histria.* Vol. 1. Bucharest, 1954.
————. *Histria.* Vol. 2. Bucharest, 1966.
   Histria, vols. 1 and 2, contain valuable contributions by various
   excavators.
Daicoviciu, Constantin; Condurachi, Emil; Nestor, Ion; and Stefan,
   Gheorghe, eds. *Istoria Romîniei.* 4 vols. Bucharest, 1960.
   An important book by a team of experts; needs updating.
Danoff, Christo M. "Tomi." In *Realencyclopädie der klassischen Al-
   tertumswissenschaft,* edited by August Pauly and Georg Wissowa.
   Supplement, vol. 9, pp. 1397–1428. Stuttgart, 1962.
Florescu, *Ghid arheologic al Dobrogei.*
Pârvan, Vasile. *Dacia.* Edited by Radu Vulpe. 5th ed. Bucharest, 1972.
   A classic, updated with very full notes; richly illustrated.
Pippidi, D. M. In *Istoria Romîniei,* edited by Constantin Daicoviciu et
   al, vol. 1, pp. 176–212.
————. "50 ans de fouilles à Histria." *Klio* 52 (1970): 355–64.
————. *I Greci nel basso Danubio.* Milan, 1971.
   The best summary of its subject; very full notes.
————. "Les inscriptions grecques de Scythie Mineure de Boeckh à nos
   jours." In *Akte des IV. Kongresses für griechische und latinische
   Epigraphik,* pp. 318–30. Vienna, 1964.
Popescu, Emilian. "Considerații asupra educației tinerelului la Histria
   in legatură cu trei inscripții inedite." *Studii și cercetări de istorie
   veche* 7 (1956): 343–63.
Preda, Constantin. *Callatis.* 2d ed. Monumentele Patriei Noastre. Bucha-
   rest, 1968.
Stoian, Iorgu. *Tomitana.*
Tafrali, Oreste. "La cité pontique de Callatis." *Arta și Arheologia*
   (Iași) 1 (1927): 17–55.
Vulpe, Radu. "Getul Burebista, conducător al întregului neam geto-dac."
   Studii și comunicări (Pitcști) 1 (1968): 35–55.
————. "Note de istorie Tomitana." *Pontice* 2 (1969): 154–67.

3. THE DACIAN HEARTLAND

Berciu, Dumitru. *Monetele în viața economică a Daciei.* Bucharest,
   1948.
Crawford, M. H. *Roman Republican Coin Hoards.* London, 1969.
   Remarkable statistics for Dacia. Additions in review by Bucur
   Mitrea, *Studii și cercetări de istorie veche* 20 (1969): 508–10.
Crisan, Ion H. *Ceramica daco-getică.* Bucharest, 1969.

————. "Necropola celtică de la Apahida." *Acta Musei Napocensis* 8 (1971): 37–53.

Daicoviciu, Constantin. "Apariția și formarea relațiilor sclavagiste în Dacia (Perioada Burebista-Decebal)." In *Istoria Rominiei,* edited by Constantin Daicoviciu et al, vol. 1, pp. 255–341.

————. "Sistemi e tecnica di costruzione militare e civile presso i Daci nella Transilvania." In *Atti del settimo Congresso Internazionale di Archeologia Classica,* vol. 3, pp. 81–86. Rome, 1961.

    Also published in Daicoviciu's *Dacica* (Cluj, 1969), pp. 101–5.

Daicoviciu, Constantin, and Daicoviciu, Hadrian. *Sarmizegethusa.* 2d ed. Monumentele Patriei Noastre. Bucharest, 1962.

Daicoviciu, Hadrian. *Dacia de la Burebista la cucerirea romană.* Cluj, 1972.

    Authoritative; summaries in French and German.

————. *Dacii.* 2d ed. Bucharest, 1972.

    Useful popular book.

Daicoviciu, Hadrian, and Glodariu, Ion. "Considerații asupra cronologie așezării dacice de la Fețele Albe." *Acta Musei Napocensis* (Cluj) 6 (1969): 465–72.

Doppelfeld, Otto, ed. *Römer in Rumänien.* Cologne, 1969.

    Exhibition catalogue, fully illustrated, with scholarly notes and references.

Gallina, Anna Z., ed. *Civiltà romana in Romania.* Rome, 1970.

    Italian edition of Doppelfeld, *Römer in Rumänien,* with a number of different illustrations.

Glodariu, Ion. "Importuri romane in cetățile dacice din Munții Orăștiei." *Apulum* 7 (1968): 353–67.

Macrea, Mihail; Floca, Octavian; Lupu, Nicolae; Berciu, Ion. *Cetăți dacice din sudul Transilvaniei.* Monumentele Patriei Noastre. Bucharest, 1966.

Preda, Constantin. *Monedele Geto-Dacilor.* Biblioteca de Arheologie, vol. 19. Bucharest, 1973.

Protase, Dumitru. *Riturile funerare la Daci și Daco-Romani.* Biblioteca de Arheologie, vol. 16. Bucharest, 1971.

Rusu, Mircea. "Das keltische Fürstengrab von Ciumești in Rumänien." *Bericht der Römisch-Germanischen Kommission des Deutschen Archäologischen Instituts* 50 (1969): 239–65.

————. *Mormînt de căpetenie celtică de la Ciumești.* Baia Mare, 1970.

Vulpe, Radu. *Așezări getice din Muntenia.* Monumentele Patriei Noastre. Bucharest, 1966.

————. "Les Gètes de la rive gauche du Bas-Danube et les Romains." *Dacia*, n.s. 4 (1960): 309–32.

————. *Piroboridava*. Bucharest, 1931.

Winkler, Judita. *Contribuții numismatice la istoria Daciei*. Studii și cercetări științifice, ser. 3, vol. 6, pp. 3–181. Cluj, 1955.

Zaharia, N.; Petrescu-Dumbovița, Mircea; and Zaharia, Emilia. *Așezările din Moldova*. Bucharest, 1970.

Zirra, Vlad. "Beiträge zur Kenntnis des keltischen La Tène in Rumänien." *Dacia*, n.s. 15 (1971): 171–238.
    Authoritative on Celts in Romania.

————. *Un cimitir celtic în nord-vestul României*. Satu Mare, 1967.

4. THE ROMAN CONQUEST: A COLUMN AND A TROPHY

Antonescu, Theohari. *Le trophée d'Adamclisi*. Iași, 1905.

Baradez, Jean. "Le trophée d'Adamklissi témoin de deux politiques et de deux stratégies." *Apulum* 9 (1971): 505–22.

Barbu, V. *Adamclisi*. Monumentele Patriei Noastre. Bucharest, 1965.

Cichorius, Conrad. *Die Reliefs der Traianssäule*. 4 vols. Berlin, 1896–1900.

Daicoviciu, Constantin, and Daicoviciu, Hadrian. *Columna lui Traian*. 2d ed. Bucharest, 1968.

Daicoviciu, Hadrian. *Dacii*.

Degrassi, Attilio. "La via seguita de Traiano nel 105 per recarsi nella Dacia." *Rendiconti della Pontificia Accademia Romana di Archeologia* 22 (1946–47): 167–83.

Florescu, F. B. *Monumentul de la Adamclisi*. 2d ed. Bucharest, 1961.
    Monumental; very fully illustrated. German edition: *Das Siegesdenkmal von Adamklissi* (Bonn, 1965).

Florescu, Radu. *Ghid arheologic al Dobrogei*.

Gallina, Anna Z., ed. *Civiltà romana in Romania*.

Lehmann-Hartleben, Karl. *Die Traianssäule*. 2 vols. Berlin-Leipzig, 1926.

Paribeni, Roberto. *Optimus Princeps*. 2 vols. Messina, 1926–27.

Patsch, Carl. *Der Kampf um den Donauraum unter Domitian und Traian*. Sitzungsberichte der kaiserlichen Akademie der Wissenschaften, philosophische-historische Klasse, vol. 217. Vienna-Leipzig, 1937.
    Fundamental.

Petersen, Enrst. *Trajans dakische Kriege, nach dem Säulenrelief erzählt*. 2 vols. Leipzig, 1899–1903.

Rădulescu, Adrian. *Monumentul triumfal de la Adamclisi.* Constanţa, 1972.
Romanelli, Pietro. *La Colonna Traiana.* Rome, 1942.
Rossi, Lino. *Trajan's Column and the Dacian Wars.* London, 1971.
  Full illustrations, poorly reproduced.
Tocilescu, Grigore; Benndorf, Otto; and Niemann, Georg. *Monumentul de la Adamklissi: Tropaeum Traiani.* Vienna, 1895.
Tudor, Dumitru. *Oltenia romană.* 3d ed. Bucharest, 1968.
  Exhaustive; contains Supplementum Epigraphicum.
———. *Podurile romane de la Dunărea de Jos.* Bucharest, 1971.
Turcan-Deleani, M. "Les monuments representés sur la colonne Trajane, schématisme et réalisme." *Mélanges d'archéologie et d'histoire de l'Ecole française de Rome* 70 (1958): 149–76.
Vulpe, Radu, and Barnea, Ion. *Din istoria Dobrogei.* Vol. 2, pp. 84–116. Bucharest, 1968.
  On Trajan's campaign in Dobruja and the Trophy.

5. DACIA UNDER ROMAN RULE: A.D. 106–271

Bărcălilă, Alexandru. *Une ville daco-romaine: Dobreta.* Bucharest, 1932.
Bichir, Gheorghe. "La civilisation des Carpes (IIe-IIIe siècle de n.è.) à la lumière des fouilles archéologiques de Poiana-Dulceşti, de Butnăreşti et de Pădureni." *Dacia,* n.s. 11 (1967): 177–224.
———. *Cultura Carpică.* Biblioteca de Arheologie, vol. 20. Bucharest, 1973.
Chirilă, Eugen; Gudea, Nicolae; Lucăcel, Vasile; and Pop, Constantin. *Castrul roman de la Bucium.* Zalău, 1972.
Christescu, Vasile. *Istoria militară a Daciei romane.* Bucharest, 1937.
———. *Viaţa economică a Daciei romane.* Piteşti, 1929.
Daicoviciu, Constantin. "Dacia Capta." *Klio* 38 (1960): 174–84.
Daicoviciu, Constantin, and Daicoviciu, Hadrian. *Ulpia Traiana.* 2d ed. Monumentele Patriei Noastre. Bucharest, 1966.
Daicoviciu, Hadrian, and Glodariu, Ion. "Un castru roman în regiunea cetăţilor dacice din Munţii Orăştiei." In *Lucrări ştiinţifice: Istoria— ştiinţe social—pedagogie,* pp. 17–30. Oradea, 1971.
Doppelfeld, Otto, ed. *Römer in Rumänien.*
Enciclopedia di arte antica classica. 7 vols. Rome, 1958–66.
  Articles on individual sites.
Floca, Octavian. "O nouă villa suburbană în hotarul Sarmizegethusei." *Sargetia* 1 (1937): 25–43.
———. "Pagus Micensis." *Sargetia* 5 (1968): 49–57.

Floca, Octavian, and Vasiliev, Valentin. "Amfiteatrul militar de la Micia." *Sargetia* 5 (1968): 121–52.

Florescu, Gregore. "Mălăești" and "Drajna de Sus." In *Omagiu lui Constantin Daicoviciu,* edited by Mihail Macrea, pp. 225–32. Bucharest, 1960.

Glodariu, Ion. "Sarmizegethusa Dacică în epoca romană." *Acta Musei Napocensis* 2 (1965): 119–33.

Gudea, Nicolae. "Limesul roman in zona castrului de la Bologa." *Acta Musei Napocensis* 8 (1971): 507–30.

Kruglikova, I. T. "Dacia provincia romană." *Analele roman-sovietice* (1956), pp. 63–93.

Macrea, Mihail. "Santierul arheologic Sf.-Gheorghe-Brețcu, 1950." *Studii și cercetări de istorie veche* 2 (1951): 287–96, 304–6.

———. *Viața în Dacia romană.* Bucharest, 1969.
    Fundamental; exhaustive documentation.

Macrea, Mihail, and Tudor, Dumitru. In *Istoria Rominiei,* edited by Constantin Daicoviciu et al, vol. 1, pp. 345–476.

Marsigli, L. F. *Danubius Pannonico-Mysicus: Observationibus Geographicis, Astronomicis, Hydrographicis, Historicis, Physicis Perlustratus.* 6 vols. Amsterdam and The Hague, 1726.

Popescu, Emilian, and Popescu, Eugenia. "Castrul roman Jidava-Cîmpulung." *Studii și comunicări* (Pitești) 1 (1968): 67–79.

Protase, Dumitru. "Berzobis." *Acta Musei Napocensis* 4 (1967): 47–72.

Stefan, Gheorghe. "Le camp romain de Drajna-de-Sus." *Dacia* 11–12 (1945–47): 115–44.

Tudor, Dumitru. *Drobeta.* Monumentele Patriei Noastre. Bucharest, 1965.

———. *Istoria sclavajului în Dacia romană.* Bucharest, 1957.
    Fundamental; Marxist bias; summaries in Russian and French.

———. *Oltenia romană.*

———. *Orase, tîrguri, și sate în Dacia romană.* Bucharest, 1968.

———. *Răscoale și atacuri "barbare" în Dacia romană.* Bucharest, 1957.

———. *Romula.* Monumentele Patriei Noastre. Bucharest, 1968.

Vulpe, Radu. "Angustia." In *Omagiu lui C. Giurescu,* pp. 551–59. Bucharest, 1944.

Winkler, Judita; Vasiliev, Valentin; Chițu, L.; and Borda, A. " 'Villa rustica' de la Aiud." *Sargetia* 5 (1968): 59–85.
    Contains useful survey of Dacian villae rusticae in general.

Zagorit, C. *Castrul roman de la Mălăești.* Ploiești, 1940.

6. DOBRUJA, 125 B.C.–A.D. 275

Adamesteanu, Dinu. "Argamum," "Axiopolis," "Capidava," and "Carsium." In *Enciclopedia di arte antica classica.*

Barnea, Ion. *Dinogetia.* Monumentele Patriei Noastre. Bucharest, 1969.

———. "Noviodunum." In *Enciclopedia di arte antica classica.*

Barnea, Ion; Stefan, Gheorghe; and Mitrea, Bucur. "Săpăturile de salvare de la Noviodunum." *Materiale și cercetări arheologice* 4 (1957): 155–74.

Barnea, Ion; Stefan, Gheorghe; Mitrea, Bucur; Comșa, Eugen; and Comșa, Maria. "Săpăturile de salvare de la Noviodunum." *Materiale și cercetări arheologice* 5 (1959): 461–73.

Betz, Artur. "Troesmis." In *Realencyclopädie der klassischen Altertumswissenschaft,* edited by August Pauly and Georg Wissowa, vol. 13A, pp. 591–96. Stuttgart, 1939.

Bordenache, Gabriella. "Ibida." In *Enciclopedia di arte antica classica.*

Canarache, Vasile. *Tomis.*

Condurache, Emil. *Histria.*

Condurache, Emil, and Daicoviciu, Constantin. *Roumanie.* Archaeologia Mundi. Geneva, 1972.
     Popular survey by experts; fully illustrated; many color plates.

Danoff, Christo M. "Tomi."

Doritiu, Emilia. "Ulmetum." In *Enciclopedia di arte antica classica.*

Florescu, Radu. *Capidava.* Monumentele Patriei Noastre. Bucharest, 1965.

———. *Ghid arheologic al Dobrogei.*

Harțuche, N. "Un car le luptă descoperit în regiunea Dobrogei." *Apulum* 6 (1967): 231–57.

Pârvan, Vasile. *Dacia,* ed. Vulpe.

Pippidi, D. M. In *Istoria Romîniei,* vol. 1, pp. 176–212.

———. *Contribuții la istoria veche a României.* 2d ed. Pp. 464–80, 534–46. Bucharest, 1967.
     Important articles; full bibliography; many illustrations.

———. *I Greci nel basso Danubio.*

———. "In jurul datei tratatului Roma-Callatis," *Studii clasice* 15 (1973): 57–67.

Preda, Constantin. *Callatis.*

Stoian, Iorgu. "De nouveau sur la plainte des paysans du territoire d'Histria." *Dacia,* n.s. 3 (1959): 369–90.

———. "O inscripție inedită din Histria." *Studii și cercetări de istorie veche* 2 (1951): 137–57.

Villagers' complaint under Antoninus Pius.
Vulpe, Radu. In Vulpe and Barnea, *Din istoria Dobrogei,* vol. 2, pp. 13–283.
　Fundamental.
———. "Salsovia." In *Enciclopedia di arte antica classica.*

7. DACIA AND MOESIA DURING THE LATE EMPIRE

Adamesteanu, Dinu. "Argamum," "Axiopolis," "Capidava," and "Carsium."
Barbu, V. *Adamclisi.*
Barnea, Ion. *Dinogetia.*
———. In Vulpe and Barnea, *Din istoria Dobrogei,* vol. 2, pp. 369–502.
———. "O casă romană tîrzie de la Dinogetia." *Studii şi cercetări de istorie veche* 20 (1969): 245–66.
Betz, Artur. "Troesmis."
Brown, David. "The Brooches in the Pietroasa Treasure." *Antiquity* 46 (1972): 111–16.
Canarache, Vasile. *L'édifice à mosaïque de Tomi.* Constanţa, n.d.
———. *Tomis.*
Condurachi, Emil. *Histria.*
Daicoviciu, Constantin, and Daicoviciu, Hadrian. *Ulpia Traiana.*
Danoff, Christo M. "Tomi."
Diaconu, Gheorghe. *Tîrgsor.* Biblioteca de Arheologie, vol. 8. Bucharest, 1968.
Doritiu, Emilia. "Ulmetum."
Dunăreanu-Vulpe, Ecaterina. *Tezaurul de la Pietroasa.* Bucharest, 1967.
Florescu, Grigore. *Capidava.* Monografie arheologică, vol. 1. Bucharest, 1958.
Florescu, Radu. *Ghid arheologic al Dobrogei.*
Macrea, Mihail. *Viaţa în Dacia romană.*
Odobescu, Alexandru. *Le trésor de Petrossa.* 2 vols. Leipzig, 1889–1900.
Petre, Aurelian. "Cultura Sîntana-de-Mureş în Scythia Minor." *Studii şi cercetări de istorie veche* 15 (1964): 59–80.
———. "Quelques données archéologique concernant la continuité de la population et de la culture romano-byzantines dans la Scythie Mineure aux VIe et VIIe siècles de nôtre ère." *Dacia,* n.s. 7 (1963): 317–53.
———. "Săpăturile de la Piatra Frecăţei." *Materiale şi cercetări arheologice* 8 (1962): 565–89.
Preda, Constantin. *Callatis.*

Preda, Constantin, and Nubar, H. *Histria*. Vol. 3. Bucharest, 1973.
    Contains catalogue of Greek and Roman coins excavated at Histria
    since 1914.
Protase, Dumitru, and Horedt, Kurt. "Ein volkerwanderungszeitlicher
    Schatzfund aus Cluj-Someșeni." *Germania* 48 (1970): 85–98.
Tudor, Dumitru. *Drobeta*.
————. *Orase, tîrguri, și sate în Dacia romană*.
————. *Podurile romane de la Dunărea de Jos*.
————. *Sucidava*.
Vulpe, Radu. In Vulpe and Barnea, *Din istoria Dobrogei*.

8. RELIGION, ARTS, AND CRAFTS

Barnea, Ion. In Vulpe and Barnea, *Din istoria Dobrogei*.
Bordenache, Gabriella. *Sculture greche e romane nel Museo Nazionale
    di Antichità*.
Canarache, Vasile. *Le musée d'archéologie Constantza*. Constanța, 1967.
Christescu, Vasile. *Viața economică a Daciei romane*.
Coja, Marie "Activitatea meșteșugărească la Histria în sec. VI-I î.e.n."
    Studii și cercetări de istorie veche 13 (1962): 19–45.
Doppelfeld, Otto, ed., *Römer in Rumänien*.
Dragomir, I. T. "Două baseoreliefuri dionasiace descoperite la Făgărașul
    Nou (Hîrșova)." *Studii și cercetări de istorie veche* 13 (1962): 421–
    29.
Ferri, Silvio. *Motivi ornamentali dell' arte romana del mezzo e basso
    Danubio*. Rome, 1933.
Florescu, Grigore. "I monumenti funerari della Dacia inferiore."
    Ephemeris Dacoromana 4 (1930): 72–148.
————. *I monumenti funerari della Dacia superiore*. Bucharest, 1942.
Florescu, Radu. *L'art des Daces*. Bucharest, 1968.
Gallina, Anna Z., ed. *Civiltà romana in Romania*.
Gramatopol, Mihail. "Optimo Principi." *Apulum* 7 (1968): 369–79.
Hanfmann, George M. *Classical Sculpture*. History of Western Sculp-
    ture, vol. 1. New York and London, 1967.
————. *Roman Art: A Modern Survey of the Art of Imperial Rome*.
    New York, 1964.
Jones, L. W. *The Cults of Dacia*. Berkeley, 1929.
Macrea, Mihail. "Le culte de Sabazius en Dacie." *Dacia*, n.s. 3 (1959):
    325–39.
————. "Cultele germanice în Dacia." *Anuarul Institutului de Studii
    clasice* (Cluj) 5 (1944–48): 219–63.

————. *Viața în Dacia romană.*

Maxim, Alexandru. "Un depozit de unelte dacice pentru exploatarea sării." *Acta Musei Napocensis* 8 (1971): 457–63.

Popa, A. I. "O nouă inscripție închinată zeiței Isis la Apulum." *Studii și cercetări de istorie veche* 13 (1962): 147–52.

Popa-Lisseanu, Gheorghe. *Tăblițe cerate descoperite în Transilvania.* Bucharest, 1890.

Popescu, Dorin O. "Le cult d'Isis et de Sérapis en Dacie." *Mélanges de l'Ecole roumaine en France* (1927), pp. 159–209.

Scorpan, Constantin. *Cavalerul trac.* Constanța, 1967.

————. *Representări bacchice.* Constanța, 1968.

Tudor, Dumitru. *Corpus Monumentorum Religionis Equitis Danubiani.* Vol. 1. Leiden, 1969.

————. "Jupiter Dolichenus în Dacia inferioară." *Apulum* 4 (1961): 14–19.

Vermaseren, M. J. *Corpus Monumentorum et Inscriptionum Religionis Mithraicae.* Vol. 2. The Hague, 1960.

INDEX

A

Adamclisi, Trajanic trophy at, 71, 80, 95, 97–105, 202. *See also* Tropaeum Traiani

Ad Mediam, best-preserved Roman camp, 133

Aegean basin, Neolithic statuettes possibly from, 6, 7

Aegyssus, barbarian attacks on, 147

Aelius Catus, Sex., Roman general, 47, 49, 146

Agighiol, tomb of Thracian prince at, silver treasure, 27–29

Aiton, villa rustica, 112n, 126

Aiud, villa rustica, 112n

Aizis, Roman camp, 76

Alba Iulia, 67, 68, 123; museum, 132. *See also* Apulum

Alburnus Maior, 126, 206

Alexander the Great, 33, 47, 48

Alexander Severus, Roman emperor, 111, 114, 115, 154–55

Amber, 17

Amorgos, harper from, 6

Ampelum: gold rush town, 125, 131, 132; Bedouin wife at, 132

Amphitheaters, at Ulpia Traiana, Porolissum, Micia, 111–12

Anastasius, Byzantine emperor: rebuilds Dinogetia, 169; dates Callatis basilica, 181

Angustia: Domitianic diploma from, 139; abandoned under Commodus, 139; military road to Cumidava, 142

Antonines: rebuild camps in stone, 136; make Troesmis a municipium, 182

Antoninus Pius, Roman emperor: repairs Ulpia Traiana amphitheater, 112; rebuilds Porolissum camp in stone, 129; and Citera, 130; diploma of, at Răcari, 142; Dobruja's apogee under, 152

Antonius Hybrida, C., proconsul, 145

Apahida: Celtic cremation cemetery at, 51; villa rustica, 112n

Aphrodite, cult of: at Callatis, 39; at Tomis, 200

Apollo: at Histria, 32; at Callatis, 40; of Aquae, 188

Apollodorus of Damascus: possible creator of Trajan's Column, 74; bridge at Drobeta, 86, 115

Apulum: site described, 123–25; survival till Theodosius I, 163; Isis in, 190. *See also* Alba Iulia

Apuseni Mountains, gold mines in, 68

Aquae, 188

Aquincum, 129

Archaeology, and man's indestructibility, 210

Arcidava: forty-acre Roman camp at, 76; Bavarian cohort at, 133. *See also* Vărădia

Argedava. *See* Popești

Aristocracy, Roman support of, 107

Aristotle, 32

Arrubium, Trajanic fort: on Danube limes, 150; honors Severans, 153

Artemis: at Histria, 32; at Callatis, 39

Art Nouveau, 12

Arutela, Roman camp, 139, 141

Arval Brethren, 73, 86

Astarte, and Venus, 190

Atargatis: at Romula, 122; equated with Venus, 190

Athanaric, king of Visigoths, makes peace with Valens, 178

Athena, cult of: at Callatis, 39

Athenian Empire, 32

H

Hăbăşeşti, 210; site described, 13–15
Hadrian, Roman emperor, 211; on
Trajan's Column, 75; partially
dismantles Dobruja bridge, 88;
peacemaker, 108; Ulpia Traiana
prospers under, 112, 114; makes
Drobeta a municipium, 116; also
Romula, 121; visits Napoca, and
makes it municipium, 127;
abandons certain Dacian camps,
139; buys off Roxolani, 139; builds
Rădăcineşti, 139; rebuilds Răcari,
142; commands legion under
Domitian, 151; in Trajan's Dacian
Wars, 151; visits Dobruja, 151;
pax Romana under, 151; Pontic
cities honor, 151; subsidizes Sar-
matians, 151; recruits Dobrujan
troops, 151; Dobruja Romanized
under, 151; abandons Tîrgşor, 167
Hallstatt period, 19
Hapsburg(s), 53, 107, 115
Harghita, 15
Heraclea Pontica, 37, 38, 39
Heracles, 38. See also Hercules
Herculaneum, 109
Hercules, 187
Hermes: at Histria, 32; at Tomis,
176
Herodotus, historian, 45
Highwaymen, 134
Hîrşova. See Carsium
Histria, 42; site described, 21–34;
Ionian constitution, 23; silted harbor, 25; necropolis, 26, 45; cults,
30, 32; politics, 32; Philip II,
Alexander, Lysimachus at, 33; edu-
cation at, 34; hard times, 34; joins
Callatis against Tomis, 40; coins
of, at Costeşti, 58; at Bărboşi, 70;
possible treaty with Rome, 145;
"second founding," 146; fishing
rights, 150; Antonine buildings,
152; honors Caracalla and Macrinus, 154; Severus Alexander and
Maximinus Thrax, 155; market,
158; sacked, 158–59; survives to
Heraclius, 163, 184; late imperial
phase, 184; classical Greek tradition at, 199; history summarized,
210. See also Pontic cities
Hobiţa, villa rustica, 113–14
Horedt, Kurt, 66n
Huns: sack Dinogetia, 169, and
Ulmetum, 174

I

Ialomiţa River, 48, 150
Iazygian embassy to Trajan, 88
Ibida, she-wolf, 155
Iglita. See Troesmis
Ilişua, Roman camp, 137–38
Illyrian dagger, at Popeşti, 49
Inlăceni, Roman camp, 138
Intaglio, at Romula, 122, 208
Interpretatio Romana, 187
Ionians, 21, 23, 25
Iron Age, 15, 19
Iron Curtain, 3
Iron Gates, 73
"Iron Gates of Transylvania," 79
Isaccea. See Noviodunum
Isis: at Romula, 122; at Tomis, 158,
194; in Dacian cities, 190
Isocrates, rhetorician, 39
Izvoare, 10

J

Jidava, Roman camp, 142
Julia Mammaea, honored by Tomis,
155
Julius Caesar, C., 53
Jupa. See Tibiscum
Jupiter Dolichenus, at Răcari, 190
Justinian, Roman emperor: Dobruja
flowers under, 150; Danube forts
of, 163; Code, 163; rebuilds and
renames Drobeta, 165; rebuilds
Sucidava citadel, 166; and Ca-